TRADES BIBLE
FOR
CANDLESTICKS

The Best Course for Trading Candlestick Patterns

Ted O. Wise

TABLE OF CONTENTS

INTRODUCTION

The Candlestick trading book is one of the most effective trading strategies in history. It was designed by Homma Munehisa. The father of candlestick chart patterns. This trader is recognized to be the most successful trader in history, he was renowned as the God of markets in his days, and his discovery earned him more than $10 billion in today's money.

I have spent 10 years creating, testing, organizing, and regularly updating this technique to create my current version, which is recognized to be the easiest and most rewarding trading system.

The Candlestick trading bible is the trading system that is going to finally take your trading to where it should be, consistent, profitable, easy, and needing very little time and effort. This trading approach is based on Japanese candlestick patterns in combination with technical analysis.

All you have to do is to spend as much time as you can to perfect the strategy that I am going to reveal to you and use it to trade in any financial market. Learning Japanese candlestick is like learning a new language. Imagine you obtain a book which is written in a foreign language, you peek at the pages but you gain nothing from what is written.

The same thing when it comes to financial markets. If you don't know how to grasp Japanese candlesticks, you will never be able to trade the market. Japanese candlesticks are the language of financial markets. If you gain the skill of reading charts, you will grasp what the market is saying to you, and you will be able to make the proper pick at the ideal time.

The simple-to-follow tactics outlined in this article will give you profit-earning ways that may be swiftly comprehended. More crucially, comprehending the notions of market psychology driving the candlestick strategy will shift your entire trading psych permanently.

The Candlestick trading book has already revealed itself. Fortunes have been made utilizing the Japanese candlestick techniques. I commend you for taking the first step in your trading education, you are on the suitable path to become a better trader.

However, this is basically only the beginning of your trading career, after reading this eBook, the actual work begins. Don't read this eBook excessively rapidly, this is not a book, you should take your time to assimilate all the thoughts I presented, take your notes, and go back from time to time to analyze the strategies I supplied to you.

Remember, this is an educational book that will teach you professional tactics on how to make money trading financial markets. If you gain the talents that I shared with you here, you will revolutionize your life and the lives of people around you.

OVERVIEW

The eBook is broken into the following sections:

1- Candlesticks Anatomy

Just like persons, candlesticks have diverse body proportions, and when it comes to trading, it's crucial to check out the bodies of candlesticks and appreciate the psychology behind them. That's what you will study in this part.

2- Candlestick Patterns

Candlestick patterns are a major aspect of technical analysis, candlestick patterns occur because human actions and emotions are patterned and consistently repeated. In this chapter, you will learn how to detect the most famous candlestick patterns, the psychology underpinning their development, and what they mean when they occur in the market.

3- The Market Structure

In this part, you will learn how to recognize trending markets, range markets, and unstable markets. You will learn how these markets operate and how to trade them efficiently. You will also learn how to draw support and resistance, and trendlines.

4- A Top-Down Analysis And Time Frames

Multiple time frame study is quite crucial for you as a price action trader, in this component, you will discover how to investigate the market utilising the top-down analysis strategy.

5- Trading Techniques and Tactics

In this chapter you will learn how to trade the market applying four price action trading strategies:

- The pin bar approach

- The enveloping bar strategy
- The inner bar strategy

- The inner bar fake breakout approach

Trades samples

I strongly urge you to master the previous sections before continuing to this region, since if you don't comprehend the fundamentals, you will not be able to employ these tactics as effectively as they would be.

In this chapter, you will learn how to identify high probability setups in the market, and how to utilize these candlestick patterns in trending markets and range markets to enhance your earnings.

6- Money Management

In this part, you will learn how to construct a money management and risk control strategy that will enable you to keep your trading capital and become consistently successful.

CHAPTER ONE

THE HISTORY OF CANDLESTICKS

Candlesticks have been around a lot longer than anything analogous in the Western world.

The Japanese were looking at charts as far back as the 17th century, but the oldest known charts in the US were in the late 19th century.

Rice trade had been launched in Japan in 1654, with gold, silver, and rape seed oil following soon after.

Rice markets controlled Japan at this time and the commodity became, it looked, more important than actual currency.

Munehisa Homma (aka Sokyu Honma), a Japanese rice trader born in the early 1700s, is largely recognised as being one of the early exponents of price movement.

He grasped basic supply and demand dynamics but also realized the fact that emotion had an influence on the design of price.

He sought to follow the emotion of the market players, and this study built the cornerstone of candlestick analysis.

He was exceedingly widely esteemed, to the point of being exalted to Samurai level.

The Japanese accomplished an extremely excellent job of keeping candlesticks secret from the Western world, right up until the 1980s, when suddenly there was a large cross-pollination of banks and financial organizations around the globe.

This is when Westerners suddenly gained wind of these strange charts. This was also about the time that charting in general suddenly became a lot easier, due to the widespread usage of the PC.

In the late 1980s, several Western analysts took interest in candlesticks. In the UK Michael Feeny, who was the head of TA in London for Sumitomo, began applying candlesticks in his daily job and started teaching the principles to London professionals.

In the December 1989 edition of Futures magazine Steve Nison, who was a technical analyst at Merrill Lynch in New York, published a report that demonstrated a sequence of candlestick reversal patterns and explained its predictive potential.

He went on to write a book on the topic, and a good book it is too. Thank you, Messrs Feeny and Nison.

Since then candlesticks have risen in popularity by the year, and these days they appear to be the typical pattern that most analysts work from.

Candlestick Analysis's Significance For Trading Analysis

Candlesticks are crucial to your trading analysis as it is considered as a visual depiction of what is going on in the market.

By looking at a candlestick, we may receive essential information about the open, high, low, and close values, which will give us an indicator of the price trend.

Candlesticks are versatile, they may be used alone or in combination with technical analysis tools like the moving averages, and momentum oscillators, they can be used also with technique like the Dow Theory or the Elliott wave theory.

I deploy candlesticks with support and resistance, trend lines, and other technical tools that you will learn in the next chapters.

Human conduct about money is continually impacted by fear; greed, and hope. Candlestick analysis will help us grasp these changing psychological aspects by showing us how buyers and sellers interact with each other.

Candlesticks supply more relevant information than bar charts, using them is a win-win scenario, as you may acquire all the trading signals that bar charts create with the improved clarity and extra indications given by candlesticks.

Candlesticks are utilised by most professional traders, banks, and hedge funds, these people trade millions of dollars every day, and they may alter the market whenever they chose.

They could grab your money rapidly if you don't comprehend the game.

Even if you can trade one hundred thousand dollars trading account, you can't change the market; you can't control what is occurring in the market.

Using candlestick patterns may help you comprehend what the big guys are doing, and will teach you when to enter, when to depart, and when to stay away from the market.

A Candlestick: What Is It?

Japanese candlesticks are created applying the open, high, low, and close of the predetermined time.

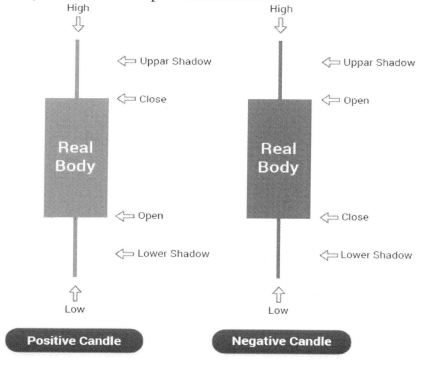

- If the close is above the open, we may assume that the candlestick is bullish which implies that the market is expanding at this moment. Bullish candlesticks are often represented as a white candlesticks.

- The bulk of trading strategies utilise white hues to allude to bullish candlesticks. But the colour isn't necessary, you may choose any shade you desire.
- The most significant are the open price and the closing price.
- If the close is below the open, we may assume that the candlestick is bearish which means that the market is declining in this session. Bearish candles are typically represented as black candlesticks. But this is not a rule.

You may discover different colours applied to distinguish between bullish and bearish candlesticks.

- The filled component of the candlestick is termed the true body.
- The small lines projecting above and below the body are called shadows.
- The tip of the upper shadow is high
- The bottom of the lower shadow is low.

Candlestick Body Sizes
Candlesticks have varied body sizes:

Long vs. Short

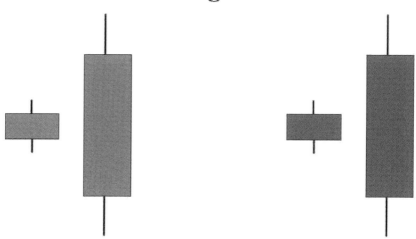

Long bodies connect to strong buying or selling pressure, if there is a candlestick in which the close is above the open with a long body, this suggests that buyers are stronger and they are gaining control of the market during this period.

Conversely, if there is a bearish candlestick in which the open is above the close with a lengthy body, this implies that the selling pressure dominates the market for this specific time period.

Short and small bodies suggest a limited purchase or selling activity.

Candlestick Shadows (Tails)

The higher and lower shadows give us essential information about the trading session.

- Upper shadows imply the session high
- Lower shadows signify the session low

Candlesticks with lengthy shadows suggest that trade activity happened considerably beyond the open and closure.

LONG SHADOWS

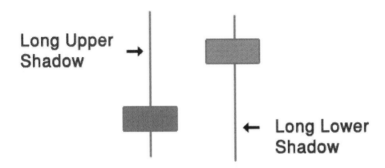

Japanese candlesticks with short shadows imply that most of the trading activity was constrained to the open and close.

A candlestick with a wider bottom shadow and a shorter top shade signifies that customers used their buying power and hiked prices. But for whatever reason, selling overwhelmed the market and drove the price back down, bringing the session to a finish at or near its opening level.

A Japanese candlestick with a lengthy bottom shadow and small top shadow symbolizes that the seller applied pressure on the price by exhibiting their washboard abs. However, for whatever reason, buyers entered the market and drove prices back up, bringing the session to a completion at the open price.

Candlestick Patterns

Candlestick patterns are among the greatest trading methods since they are obvious, easy to understand, and incredibly lucrative settings. A study has proven that candlestick patterns have a strong predictive value and may offer favorable impacts.

Since I tried hundreds of methods and trading approaches without success, I have been trading candlestick patterns for more than 20 years and I am unable to change to another strategy.

This trading method works, but be ready to lose some deals. I'm not seeking to show you the holy grail. In this game, losing is inevitable. I strongly urge you to cease trading and hunt for another company if your purpose is to uncover a strategy that will always be lucrative.

If you dwell in a foreign country and don't know the language, candlestick patterns are the language of the market. How would you manage if you couldn't even communicate? It's tough, right? The same is true in terms of commerce.

You will be able to grasp what candlestick patterns tell about market dynamics and trader behavior if you know how to examine them correctly. You will be able to better enter and depart the market at the right period thanks to this expertise.

In other words, this will help you to act differently in the market and win money by mimicking the sage.

The candlestick patterns I'm going to demonstrate to you are the most critical ones you'll confront in the market. I won't go into great detail in this chapter on how to trade them; it will be handled in the ones that follow.

What I want you to do is focus on the design and psychology of the pattern, as this will offer you the ability to recognize any pattern you confront in the marketplace and grasp what it is asking you to perform next.

If you can gain this capacity, you'll be equipped to comprehend and master the trading methods and approaches I'll show you in the coming chapters.

The Engulfing Bar Candlestick Pattern

The Engulfing bar is formed when it engulfs the candle preceding it, as its name suggests. More than one previous candle may be swallowed by the engulfing bar, but at least one candle must be consumed for it to be labelled an engulfing bar. One of the most known candlestick patterns is the bearish engulfing.

Two bodies make up this candlestick pattern:

In other words, the second body engulfs the first body since the first is smaller. Look at the picture below:

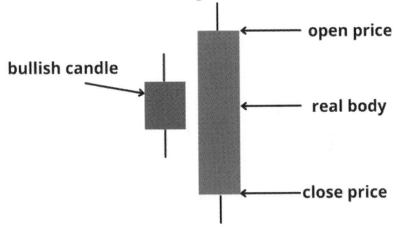

Bearish Engulfing Bar

This is how a bearish engulfing bar pattern appears on your charts; this candlestick pattern delivers crucial info regarding market bulls and bears.

A bearish engulfing bar signifies that sellers are in power of the market when it shows this pattern.

This pattern demonstrates that buyers are swallowed by sellers, which signals a trend reversal, when it occurs after a surge.

See the example below:

bearish engulfing bar

As you can see, when this price action pattern occurs during an upswing, we may be able to foresee a trend reversal since sellers are aiming to drive the market down rather than purchasers, who are still in control of the market.

You need additional technical tools to corroborate your inputs as you can't trade every bearish candlestick pattern you spot on your chart.

In the next chapters, we'll go into deeper detail addressing this. I just want you to look at your charts right now and try to spot any bearish candlestick patterns you come across.

The Bullish Engulfing Bar Pattern

The bullish engulfing bar consists of two candlesticks, the first one is the little body, and the second is the engulfing candle,

See the illustration:

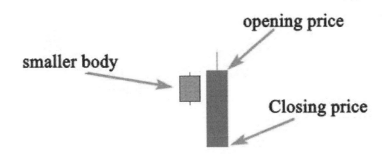

The bullish engulfing bar pattern educates us to the concept that buyers will soon take control of the market as sellers no longer have authority over it.

A bullish engulfing candle provides a continuation signal when it arises during an upswing.

The reversal is substantially more spectacular when a bullish engulfing candle comes at the bottom of a downtrend since it suggests a capitulation bottom.

See the example below:

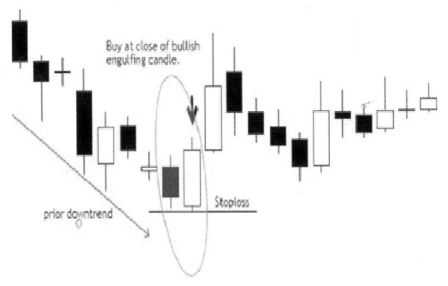

The image above makes it incredibly obvious how the market alters course once a bullish engulfing bar pattern arises.

The second body, which stands for purchase power, covered the smaller body, which indicates selling power.

The bodies' colouring is not extremely significant. It's vital that the second candlestick totally swallows the smaller one.

Don't try to trade the market using simply this price action setup; you'll need additional confluences to judge whether or not the pattern is worth trading. I'll explore this in further detail in the following chapters.

I want you to develop the skill of recognizing bearish and bullish engulfing bars on your charts straight instantly. Currently, this is the most essential period.

The Doji Candlestick Pattern

One of the most notable Japanese candlestick patterns is the doji, which tells us when the market opens and closes at the same price, demonstrating that buyers and sellers are equally hesitant and that there is no one in command of the market. See the example below:

Doji Candlestick

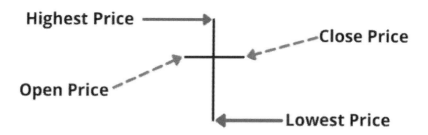

As you can see the initial price is the same as the ending price, this indicator suggests that the market didn't pick which way would follow. When this pattern occurs in an upswing or a depression, it implies that the market is likely to reverse.

See another example below to learn more:

The aforementioned image demonstrates how the market switched direction when the Doji candlestick gained shape.

The fact that the market was headed upward shows that buyers were in control of it.

The creation of the Doji candlestick signifies that sellers are able to bring prices back to their beginning levels while buyers are unable to sustain them there.

This is an evident sign that a trend reversal is probably about to occur.

Always stay in mind that a Doji implies equality and pause in the market; you will frequently observe one during moments of rest after strong swings up or down.

It is deemed a sign that a previous trend is diminishing in strength when it is detected around the bottom of the trend's apex.

Therefore, if you are already riding that trend, it is time to grab profits. If it is combined with other technical analysis signals, it may also operate as an entrance signal.

PATTERN OF THE DRAGONFLY DOJI

When the open high and close prices are the same or nearly the same, a bullish candlestick pattern called the Dragonfly Doji is generated. The longer lower tail, which reflects buyers' resistance and their determination to propel the market higher, is what defines the dragonfly Doji.

See the example below:

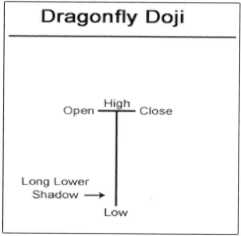

The artwork at top showcases a flawless dragonfly Doji. The trend's direction may be nearing a major turning point, as evidenced by the extended lower tail, which shows that supply and demand dynamics are achieving equilibrium. View the picture below to witness a dragonfly Doji's bullish reversal indicator.

The market was pushing the preceding support level in the chart above, which led to a sharp rejection from this zone. There is a lot of purchase interest in the area, as evidenced by the dragonfly Doji formation with the extended lower tail.

You can determine where support and demand are situated visually if you can notice this candlestick pattern on your chart. It is considered a favorable indication of a turnaround when it occurs during a downturn. To produce high probability dragonfly Doji signals in the market, you will need additional indicators and tools, as I continually mention; you cannot trade candlestick patterns alone.

Doji on a Gravestone

The Gravestone Doji, which is the dragonfly Doji's bearish twin, emerges when the prices at open and close are equal to or nearly identical. The expanded higher tail is what differentiates the Gravestone Doji from the dragonfly Doji. A sign that the market is testing a strong supply or resistance zone is the emergence of the protracted upper tail.

See the example below:

Gravestone Doji

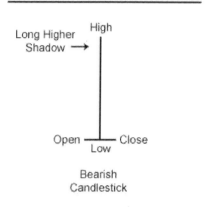

The magnificent tombstone Doji may be seen in the photos above. This pattern illustrates that buyers were successful in pushing prices substantially above the open.

Later in the day, a surplus of sellers pulled the price back down.

This is considered as a signal that bulls are losing momentum and that a reversal is imminent.

See another photo below:

The preceding chart displays a tombstone Doji at the pinnacle of an uptrend, which comes after a period of heavy bullish activity.

This candlestick pattern's appearance implies that buyers are no longer in charge of the market. This pattern needs to appear around a resistance level in order to be trustworthy. To fully grasp the signal as a trader, you will need extra details about the placement and context of the tombstone Doji. In the coming chapters, I will instruct you on this.

The Morning Star

Morning Star Pattern

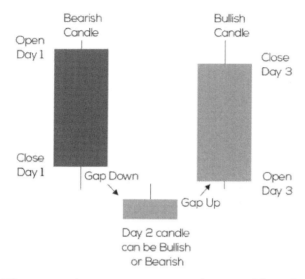

The morning star pattern is considered a bullish reversal pattern, it often occurs at the bottom of a downtrend and it consists of three candlesticks:

The first candlestick is bearish which means that sellers are still in charge of the market.

The second candle is a tiny one which signifies that sellers are in power, but they don't force the market much down and this candle may be bullish or bearish.

The third candle is a bullish candlestick that gapped up on the open and closed above the midpoint of the body of the first day, this candlestick carries a strong trend reversal indication.

The morning star pattern teaches us how buyers grabbed control of the market from sellers when this pattern emerges at the bottom of the slide at a support level that is seen as a crucial trend reversal signal.

See the image below:

READING PRICE ACTION
MORNING STAR

2. Selling pressure with decreased volatility

3. Bearish expectations failed

1. Buying pressure

The chart above lets us differentiate the morning star pattern and how it is exceptional when it is generated near the bottom of a downturn. As you can see the pattern happened within an apparent negative trend.

While the second candle produces market hesitancy, the first candle reveals the seller's advantage. Any candle, including a Doji, may be the second candle. However, in this case, the Doji candle signalled that sellers are seeking to bring the market down. The market is projected to advance as evidenced by the third bullish candle, which shows buyers seizing control from sellers.

If you can learn the structure of candlestick patterns and the psychology that drives their formations, you will be able to analyze financial markets in the same way that skilled traders analyse the market using candlestick patterns.

The Evening Star Pattern

The evening star pattern is classified as a negative reversal pattern that commonly arises at the height of an upswing.

The design consists of three candlesticks:

The first candle is bullish

The second candle is a little candlestick, it may be bullish or bearish or it may be a Doji or any other candlestick.

The third candle is a large bearish candle. In general, the evening star pattern is the bearish version of the morning star pattern.

See the example below:

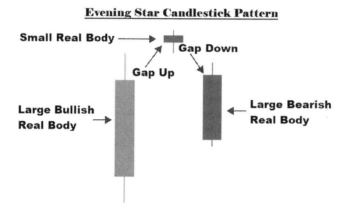

An evening star's initial portion is a bullish candle, showing that bulls are still pushing the market upward.

Everything is operating really beautifully right now. The advent of the smaller body means that although consumers are still in power, their influence has lessened.

The development of a third negative candle denotes the end of the buyer's dominance and the potential of a bearish trend reversal.

View a different graphic that highlights how the evening star might deliver a big trend reversal indicator.

The first candle in the pattern suggests a protracted push up since, as you can see, the market was headed higher.

The second candle is a short one that implies price consolidation and hesitancy. To put it another way, the trend that generated the first extended bullish candlestick is diminishing. A significantly lower final candlestick than the one before it suggests confirmation of the reversal and the commencement of a new downtrend.

The Hammer (pin bar)

The Hammer candlestick is formed when the open high and close are roughly the same price. It is typified by a long lower shadow that demonstrates the buyers' bullish rejection and their eagerness to push the market higher.

See the picture below to see what it looks like:

Hammer - (Pin Bar)

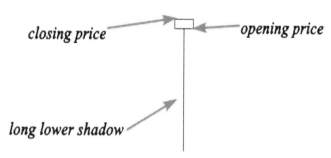

littel to no
upper shadow

closing price ——→ ←—— *opening price*

long lower shadow ——→

When it appears at the bottom of a downtrend, the hammer candlestick pattern is a reversal candlestick pattern.

This candle emerges when sellers force the market lower after it begins, but buyers turn them down, causing the market to terminate at a greater price than it started at.

See another example below:

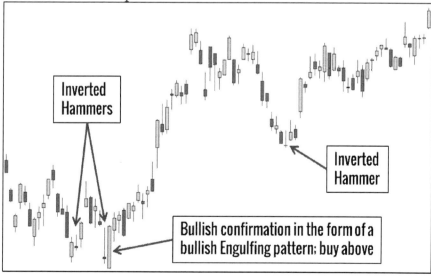

Inverted Hammers

Inverted Hammer

Bullish confirmation in the form of a bullish Engulfing pattern; buy above

As you can see, the market was heading down when the hammer (pin bar) arrived, which was a significant pattern of reversal.

The broad shadow serves as a reflection of the enormous competitive pressure from this region.

The market was being pressured lower by sellers, but at that moment, buying strength outweighed selling pressure, which triggered a trend reversal.

The psychology that underpinning the building of this pattern is the most crucial thought to know since, if you can find how and why it was produced, you will be able to forecast the market's route quite properly.

In the upcoming chapters, we'll discuss how to trade this pattern and how to filter this signal.

THE SHOOTING STAR (BEARISH PIN BAR)

The shooting formation arises when the open low, close, and price are roughly equal. This candle has a short body and a long top shadow. It is the hammer's bearish variation. Professional experts recommend that the shadow be twice as long as the person itself.

See the example below:

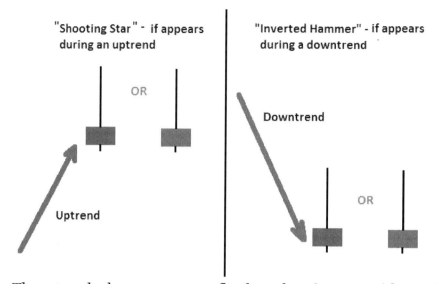

"Shooting Star" - if appears during an uptrend

OR

Uptrend

"Inverted Hammer" - if appears during a downtrend

Downtrend

OR

The artwork above portrays a flawless shooting star with a real little body and an extended shadow above it. When this pattern forms during an upswing, it offers a negative reversal indicator.

This pattern is the product of the assumption that buyers desire to push the market higher but are thwarted by selling pressure. when a resistance level is there and this candlestick forms. It should be deemed a setup with a high likelihood.

See another example below:

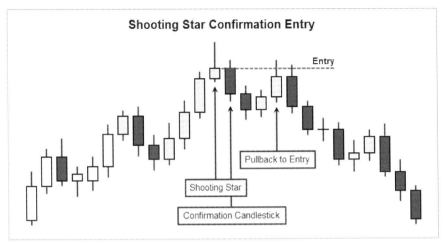

Shooting Star Confirmation Entry

In the chart above, the rising trend is approaching its finish and there is a gorgeous shooting star. The creation of this pattern marks the completion of the rising increase and the onset of a new drop.

The supply and demand zones, support and resistance levels, and technical indicators may all be utilised in connection with this candlestick pattern. The shooting star is one of the most trustworthy signs I use to enter the market since it is quite easy to discover and highly lucrative. I'll coach you through each stage of trading this price action pattern to earn money.

The Harami Pattern (the inner bar)

The two candlesticks that make up the Harami pattern—pregnant in Japanese—are viewed as a reversal and continuation pattern. A larger candle, known as the mother candle, is ignited first, followed by a smaller flame, known as the baby candle. In order for the Harami pattern to be genuine, the second candle must shut outside the first.

When this candlestick emerges at the pinnacle of an uptrend, it is recognized as a negative reversal indicator; nevertheless, when it does so at the bottom of a downtrend, it is viewed as a positive signal.

See an example below:

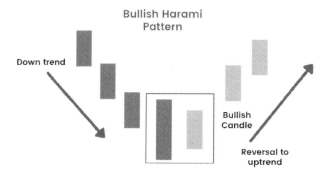

Bullish Harami
Pattern

Down trend

Bullish
Candle

Reversal to
uptrend

Bearish Harami

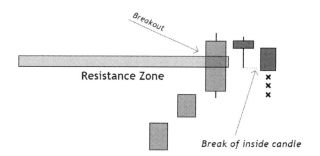

Breakout

Resistance Zone

Break of inside candle

Don't care about the colours; the key thing is that the smaller body closes inside of the first larger candle, as you can see the smaller body is totally covered by the previous mother candle. The Harami candle advises us about the market's situation of uncertainty. The market is consolidating, in various ways.

As a result, neither buyers or sellers are certain what to do, and no one is in charge of the market. This candlestick pattern is viewed as a continuation pattern that offers a good opportunity to join the trend whether it emerges during an upswing or a downswing. And it is regarded as a trend reversal whether it has happened at the height of an uptrend or the bottom of a downtrend signal.

Look at another example below:

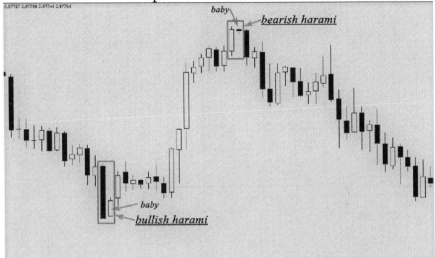

The first bullish harami pattern occurred at the bottom of a downtrend, when sellers were pushing the market down, and suddenly price started consolidating, signifying that the selling force is no longer in control of the market. You can note how the trend direction varies in the chart above.

The bearish Harami is the opposite of the bullish one; it occured at the height of an uptrend, signalling that buyers' control has ended and the start of a decline is likely. This pattern indicates a continuous indicator of the market's direction whether it comes during an upswing or a downturn.

In the coming chapters, we'll go into great detail on how to trade this pattern as a continuation or reversal pattern.

The Tweezers tops and bottoms

The bottom of the tweezer formation is recognized as a bullish reversal pattern found at the bottom of a downtrend, while the top formation is seen as a negative reversal pattern noticed at the top of an uptrend.

See the example below:

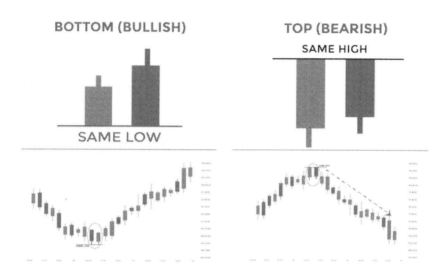

TWEZEER TOP & BOTTOM CANDLESTICK PATTERN

BOTTOM (BULLISH)   **TOP (BEARISH)**

Two candlesticks make up the tweezer's top formation: a bullish candlestick comes first, followed by a bearish candlestick. The bottom configuration of the tweezer also features two candlesticks.

A bullish candlestick is depicted after the initial bearish candle.

Therefore, we may conclude that the tweezer's bottom is the top's bullish equal.

The tweezer's top rises when buyers push the price higher during an upswing, giving us the illusion that the market is still headed upward. However, sellers stunned buyers by driving the market down and closing off the opening of the bullish candle.

If we can employ this signal in conjunction with other technical indicators, we may trade this price action pattern, which implies a bullish trend reversal.

The tweezers bottom happens during a slump when sellers drive the market lower. At the time, we believed everything was wonderful, but the following session's price closed above or virtually at the same price as the first bearish candle, signifying that buyers are on their way to defy the trend and take control of the market.

A negative reversal is likely to occur if this price movement is close to a support level.

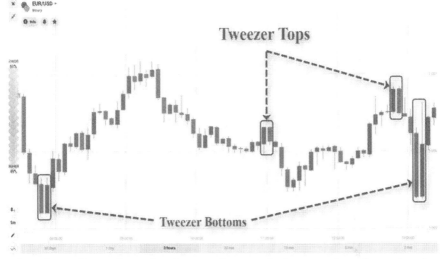

The deep low that the bears dragged the market into in the first session is seen in the chart above. However, the second session resumed where the preceding session's prices stopped and proceeded straight up, producing a reversal buy signal that you may trade provided you have extra factors that support your buying option.

Instead of focussing on a candlestick's name, seek to comprehend the psychology that went into developing it; this is more crucial. Because if you understand how it was developed, you will be able to comprehend what transpired in the market and easily estimate how the price will move in the future.

CHAPTER TWO

EXERCISE USING CANDLESTICK PATTERNS

Now that you've learned a little about Japanese candlesticks, I suppose you know how each candlestick is manufactured and the psychology behind it. Let's put your knowledge to the test and see if you can still recall every candlestick we covered by completing this homework.

Try to identify the names of the candlestick numbers and the psychology that led to their construction by looking at the graphic below.

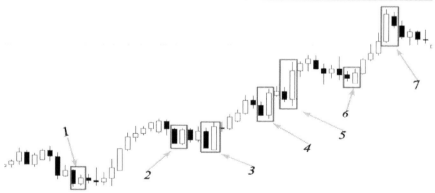

If you are able to spot these candlestick patterns and you are aware of how and why they are generated. You are heading the appropriate path. But if you continue to have issues spotting these patterns, you will need to re-study them until you feel as though you have mastered them. Let's try to answer the concerns posed by the candlestick patterns depicted on the charts above:

1: Bullish Harami pattern (inside bar)

This candlestick pattern was produced as a result of market hesitancy, suggesting that the market was consolidating during this session.

2: Bullish Tweezers

Sellers wanted to decrease the market since it was trading higher, but buyers responded more furiously. This pattern portrays the conflict between buyers and sellers to dominate the market.

3: Engulfing bar

Sellers were swamped by buyers, which demonstrates that purchasers are still set to drive the market higher.

4: Engulfing bar

5: Engulfing bar

6: Engulfing bar

7: Harami pattern

The market begins a phase of consolidation during this session, according to this trend. As a result, both buyers and sellers are unsure. Furthermore, no one is certain of the market's future.

Let's undertake a new exercise and try to detect these candlestick patterns by looking at the chart below:

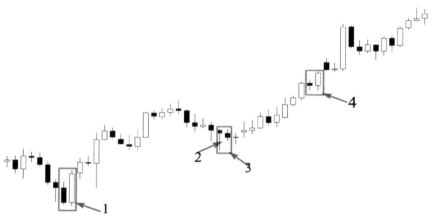

Answers:

1: Bullish engulfing bar

2: Hammer

3:(Hammer which is the large body +the little body (baby) =Harami pattern

4: Bullish engulfing bar

Please open your charts and perform this activity as many times as you need to. With more screen time and education, you'll notice that you're able to look at your charts and comprehend what the candlesticks are trying to tell you about the market. For the time being, don't worry about how to enter and exit the market; instead, take your time and strive to absorb the candlestick patterns mentioned in the past chapters.

In the following chapters, I'll give you techniques that will assist you to discover the ideal entry and exit chances employing candlestick patterns and technical analysis.

You will transform from a rookie trader who finds it challenging to profit in the market to a successful price action trader with these strategies, I promise.

THE MARKET STRUCTURE

Understanding the market structure is one of the most significant qualities you'll need as a trader as it will assist you to utilize the right price action methods under the optimum market conditions.

You won't trade all markets in the same method; instead, you need to know how they function and how traders respond. The investigation of market behavior is called the market structure. When you open your chart, you will be able to respond to these essential questions if you can master this gift.

What do people in general do? Who is in charge of the buyers or sellers on the market? What is the ideal time and place to enter or depart the market, and when should you keep away?

You will come across three basic forms of markets during your price action research: trending markets, range markets, and stormy markets. You will learn how to spot every market and how to trade it in this chapter.

1-Trending markets

Simply stated, a pattern of higher highs and higher lows in an uptrending market and lower highs and lower lows in a downtrending market represents a trending market.

See the example below:

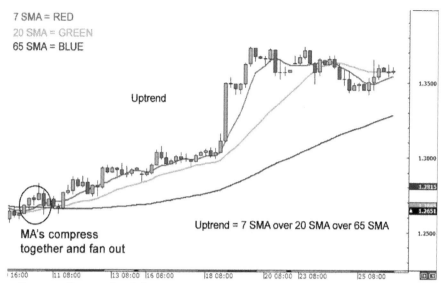

7 SMA = RED
20 SMA = GREEN
65 SMA = BLUE

Uptrend

MA's compress
together and fan out

Uptrend = 7 SMA over 20 SMA over 65 SMA

The market is building a sequence of higher highs and higher lows, as demonstrated in the sample above, which demonstrates that the market is uptrending. It is easy to determine the market direction only by looking at price movement; indicators are not necessary to indicate whether it is bullish or bearish.

Consider another instance of a bear market.

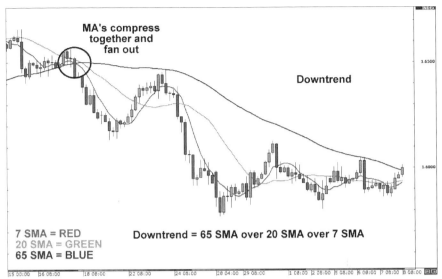

MA's compress together and fan out

Downtrend

Downtrend = 65 SMA over 20 SMA over 7 SMA

7 SMA = RED
20 SMA = GREEN
65 SMA = BLUE

Since you can see, the sample above demonstrates a bearish market as a series of higher lows and lower lows imply an apparent collapse.

Trending marketplaces are uncomplicated to locate; instead of seeking to overcomplicate your investigation, employ common sense to comprehend what the market is doing. Simply stated, a market is in an uptrend if it is making a series of higher highs and higher lows; on the other side, a market is in a downtrend if it is making a series of lower highs and lower lows.

In light of the fact that trends are anticipated to happen 30% of the time, it is vital to know how to profit from them when they are already underway.

Use larger time periods, such as the 4H, daily, or weekly timeframe, to analyze whether a market is trending or not. Never try to construct the market structure over short time periods.

How to trade trending markets:

It will be simpler for you to trade a trending market if you can spot it; if it is bullish, you will look for a buy opportunity since you must trade with the trend; and if it is bearish, you will hunt for a selling opportunity.

The difficulty remains, though, when is the best opportunity to enter a rising market?

Two major movements—the initial advance and the retracement move—define trending markets. The impulsive motion is the first movement.

See the sample below to understand what I'm talking about.

As you can see, the market is making higher highs and higher lows, signifying a bullish market. If you watch this market, you will feel it is a good time to acquire. But as you can see, there are two separate movies taking place in the market: the first is impulsive, and the second is a retreat or retracement. (Correctional action)

Professional traders are aware of how trending markets function; they always buy at the commencement of an impulsive move and collect profits at its culmination. The market moves impulsively in the trend's direction for this reason before retreating before acting impulsively again.

If you are acquainted with how trendy marketplaces function, you will learn that the best time to buy is at the start of an impulsive advance. Traders who acquire an uptrend market at the outset of a retracement move commonly get caught by experienced traders and struggle to grasp why the market hints at their stop loss before progressing in the direction they had projected. another instance of a negative trend.

The market in the graphic above is in a downtrend, so as you can see, the ideal trading approach is to sell the market as soon as an impulsive move starts.

You will lose your transaction if you try to sell during the retracement move because experienced traders will catch you.

Now that we are aware of both uptrends and downtrends, we can discern between impulsive movements and retracement moves. Knowing this is crucial information for price action traders like you.

The most significant problem, however, is learning how to spot the start of an impulsive move so that you may enter the market with professional traders at the correct period and avoid being caught by a retracement move. To forecast the start of an impulsive move in a moving market, you must master sketching support and resistance levels.

What exactly are levels of support and resistance, and how do we depict them on our charts? The next chapter will show us this in action.

Support and Resistance Levels

Support and resistance are well-known regions where buyers and sellers attain a certain level of equilibrium; they represent critical market turning moments.

When the price reverses and changes direction, support and resistance levels are formed. The price will typically respect these levels, which tend to restrain price movement unless, of course, the price explodes through them.

Support and resistance in trending markets are supplied by swing points. The previous swing point functions as a support level during an uptrend and a resistance level during a downturn.

See the sample below to learn more

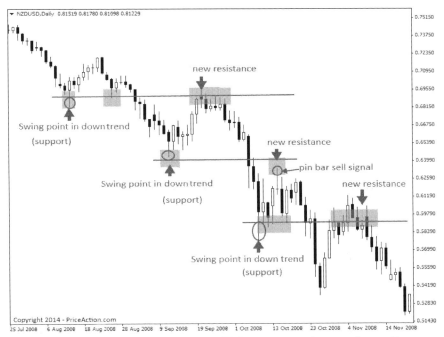

Support and resistance are well-known regions where buyers and sellers attain a certain level of equilibrium; they represent critical market turning moments.

When the price reverses and changes direction, support and resistance levels are formed. The price will typically respect these levels, which tend to restrain price movement unless, of course, the price explodes through them.

Support and resistance in trending markets are supplied by swing points. The previous swing point functions as a support level during an uptrend and a resistance level during a downturn.

See the sample below to learn more

43

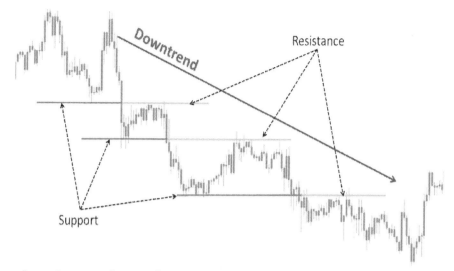

The picture above demonstrates how the market identifies resistance levels as the price moves closer to the preceding swing point (resistance level).

A swift decision is reached by the market. Understanding the price activity in a trending market may help you estimate the onset of the next impulsive move quite accurately.

By generating trend lines, one additional strategy for spotting the start of an impulsive move is doable.

You need to gain this technological knowledge as well if you desire to discover key linear support and resistance levels.

First, let me define what trend lines represent.

The price will usually choose to follow a linear level, also known as a trend line, when the market is moving and establishing new swing highs and lows.

Markets that are bullish will typically develop a linear support level, and markets that are bearish will construct a linear resistance level.

How are trend lines created?

Find at least two minimum swing points and just connect them to one another to make a reasonable trend line. Don't try to push a trend line; the levels must be obvious.

Never apply shorter time frames to build trend lines; instead, strive for unmistakable trend lines using the 4H and daily time periods.

Right now, we'll try to focus on how to draw them in a trending market; our purpose is to spot the start of impulsive moves in a trending market.

I'll go into great detail in the upcoming chapter on how to trade trend lines in tandem with our price action trading setups.

See an example of how to draw trend lines in a collapsing market.

When you can see, the market respects the trend line and, when the price gets close to it, turns around and follows the same trajectory.

Trend lines aid us anticipate the direction of the next impulsive move when the market swings in this way.

Consider another additional indicator of a growing market..

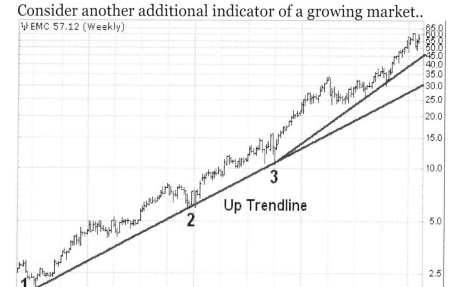

As you can see, the trend line is acknowledged by the market, and by drawing it correctly, we can forecast the next rise in price with ease.

All we can say about trending markets is that it's straightforward and easy. Now that you know that, I want you to open your charts and hunt for trending markets.

Look for prior swing points of support and resistance and try to uncover trend lines as well.

You will understand how trending markets operate with this practice. and how to anticipate market entrance with a high possibility.

The Ranging Market

Ranging markets are reasonably uncomplicated; they are sometimes referred to as sideways markets since their neutral nature gives them the sense of horizontally drifting to the right.

We may conclude that the market is growing when it frequently records greater highs and higher lows. On the flip side, we refer to the market as ranging when it stops hitting these consecutive peaks.

With prices only bouncing back and forth between the support and resistance levels, a range market swings in a horizontal pattern.

See the example below:

As you can see, the price is bouncing between a horizontal support and resistance level in the aforementioned range market chart.

Trending markets differ from range markets in that they often move by forming a pattern of higher highs and higher lows during uptrends and higher lows and lower lows during downtrends.

However, range markets often move horizontally between important levels of support and resistance. Your ability to employ the relevant price action tactics in the appropriate market scenarios will be strengthened by your comprehension of the contrasts between the two markets.

Trading ranging markets differ fundamentally from trading trending markets because ranging markets achieve equilibrium when buyers and sellers are equal and there is no leader.

Up until the range structures break out and a trending situation starts to form, this will typically stay. Major levels of support and resistance provide the ideal chance for buying and selling. Trading between markets may be done using one of three techniques. I won't get into details because I want you to learn the skill of examining your charts to detect whether the market is trending or range.

The trading approaches and tactics you will utilize to trade trending or range markets will be detailed in more depth in coming chapters. You won't be able to apply these price action strategies if you can't spot the difference between range markets and trending markets.

The initial technique for trading range markets is to wait until the price reaches the key support or resistance level, at which point you may buy at the key support level or sell at the key resistance level.

See the example below:

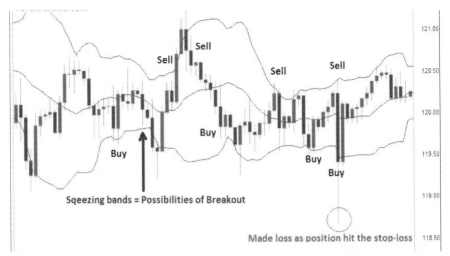

Sqeezing bands = Possibilities of Breakout

Made loss as position hit the stop-loss

As you can see, the market is presently moving horizontally, and the largest buying possibilities are placed next to the support level.

The greatest selling possibilities are situated close to the resistance level.

Waiting for the breakout from either the support level or the resistance level is the second technique for trading range markets.

You must pay attention to the boundaries when the market is ranging since no one can foretell what will happen or who will rule the market. However, when one of the participants decides to take control of the market, we will witness a breakout of the support or resistance level.

The breakout signifies that the range phase has completed, and the commencement of a new trend will take place...

See the example below:

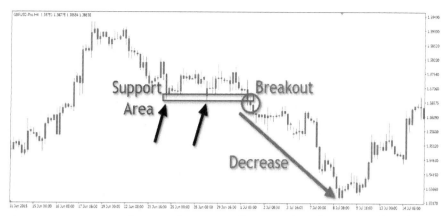

As you can see, the market was fluctuating between levels of support and resistance until suddenly the price burst beyond the barrier, marking the likely start of a trend. Therefore, following the breakout is the optimum timing to enter.

Range boundaries are repeatedly overshot, generating the appearance that a breakout is taking place. This may be highly misleading and may trap many traders that are positioned into the breakthrough. Waiting for a downturn after the breakdown of the support or resistance level is the third technique for trading range markets. For traders who opt not to participate in the breakout, the retreat presents another chance to enter the trend.

See the example below:

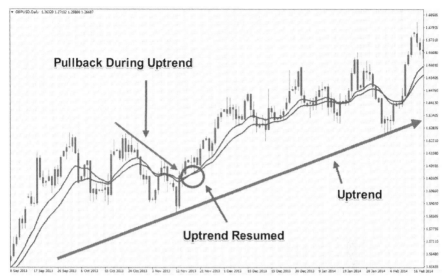

The price breaks out of the resistance level, as illustrated in the chart above, to denote the completion of the market's range phase and the initiation of a new trend.

Following the breakthrough, the market returns to retest the resistance level before it turns into support and rises higher.

If you miss the breakout, your next chance to join the buyers will be during the slump.

However, pullbacks don't always follow a breakthrough; when they do, they provide a tremendous opportunity with a favorable risk-to-reward ratio.

What you need to remember is that a ranging market alternates between trading at the support and resistance levels.

These are the critical moments that need your attention. The conclusion of the ranging phase is characterized by the breach of the support or resistance level, so you must check that the breakout is real in order to join the new trend safely.

Wait for the downturn if you fail to make the breakthrough. When that occurs, don't be reluctant to enter the market.

If you feel you can't establish the restrictions when trading range markets, always make sure the market is worth trading (support and resistance). This is a reliable sign of a chaotic market.

When you check your chart in Forex and find a lot of noise, you can't even discern whether the market is in a range or trending. These markets lack evident direction.

You must be cognizant that you are experiencing a chaotic market. When a market like this starts to perform poorly, it could drive you to feel overly emotional and doubt your trading strategies.

By merely zooming out on the daily chart and observing the bigger picture, one may identify whether a market is turbulent.

You will be able to detect whether a market is range-bound or volatile with easily with proper teaching, practice, and screen time.

Here is a good example of a choppy chart that is not worth trading.

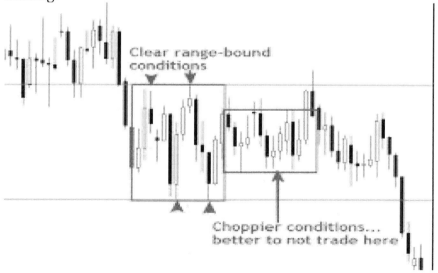

The highlighted region of the above chart's price movement is very choppy and is moving sideways within a very confined tight range, as can be observed. This is a symptom of a turbulent market that you should avoid.

If a market is choppy, in my view, it is not worth trading because, if you attempt to do so, you will lose your winnings straight away after making huge gains since markets generally consolidate after making big swings.

CHAPTER THREE

TOP-DOWN ANALYSIS AND TIME FRAMES

Your important time frames as a price action trader are the 1H, 4H, and daily.

If you try to trade pin bars or engulfing bars in the 5-minute time frame, you will lose money as there is a lot of noise on smaller time frames and the market will give a lot of false signals thanks to the fierce struggle between the bulls and bears. Price action operates on larger time horizons.

In addition, no skilled price action trader examines his charts using merely a one-time frame. You may be conscious of the expression "top and down analysis," which refers to starting with broader time frames to comprehend the overall picture before switching to smaller ones to decide whether to buy or sell the market.

Assuming you wish to trade the 4h chart, you must first look at the weekly chart before proceeding on to the daily chart. If the weekly and daily chart analysis align with the 4h chart, you may then decide which trade to make.

Additionally, you must first look at the daily chart if you want to trade the 1H chart. This is a vital step for price action traders to take as it will allow you to keep focused on high-probability price action signals and help you avoid low-probability trading setups.

We always begin with the lengthier duration in our top-down analysis and check for the following details:

The most critical support and resistance levels: these areas signify market turning points; if you can detect them on the weekly chart, you'll be able to foresee what will happen when the price approaches them on the 4h chart. Therefore, you will select whether to acquire, sell, or ignore the market indicators.

The market structure: You may find from the weekly study if the market is in a range or experiencing volatility, as well as whether it is moving up or down. Generally speaking, you will be aware of what the big investors are doing. And you'll try to find out how to employ my price action strategies to follow them throughout shorter time periods.

The preceding candle: The last candle on the weekly chart is vital because it summarizes the week's events and delivers key hints about future market swings. When you identify these locations on the weekly chart, proceed to the daily chart or the 4-hour chart and make an effort to gather data such as:

The situation of the market: what is it doing over 4 hours, is it moving upward or lower, is it fluctuating, or is it in a volatile state? What are the four-hour or daily key levels that are most important: These could be trend lines, supply and demand zones, or regions of support and resistance.

A candlestick pattern that indicates a price movement indicator can assist you determine whether to buy or sell the market. This could be an inner bar, a pin bar, or an encircling bar.

Let me present an example to highlight the significance of utilizing top-down analysis in your trading technique and what will happen if you don't look at the broader time frame before proceeding to your primary chart.

Take a look at the example below:

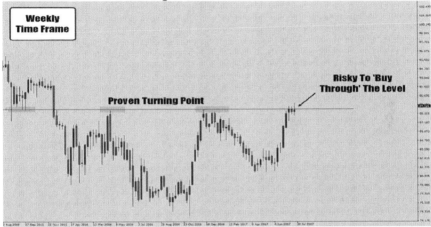

We have received two crucial data points that will assist us to select what to do in the daily time period, as you can see in the weekly chart above.

The market is heading nearing a large weekly resistance level, which will imply a difficult moment for the market.

The price was promptly rejected as it hit this important resistance level, which implies that there are sellers there and that they are willing to short the market. This offers the second piece of information.

The formation of the inner bar false breakout patterns, which predict a reversal, validates our theory.

Let's now evaluate the daily period to learn what is happening in the market:

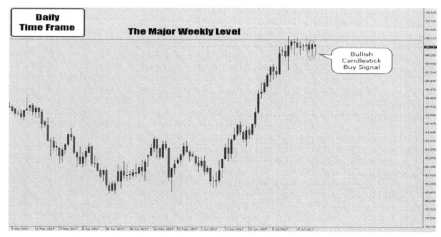

We can obviously discern a pin bar candlestick pattern on the daily chart, which implies a bullish trend.

If you merely focus on one time period when making your trading decision, you will acquire the market because there is a clear pin bar signal. However, if you looked at the weekly chart, you would observe that the market is hitting a very significant critical level that would restrict it from climbing further. Therefore, if there is a clear indication, it is preferable to consider selling the market rather than acquiring it.

Look at what transpired after that:

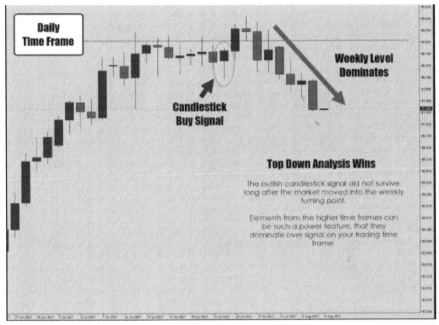

As you can see, the weekly resistance level was a critical turning point that altered the market trend, demonstrating that top-down analysis is advantageous while the pin bar candlestick indication is useless. I strongly recommend you to discontinue trading if you intend to trade price movement solely on a one-time frame because you will end up losing your complete trading account and you will never become a successful trader.

Trading against trends may be incredibly lucrative as well, but without top-down research, you run the possibility of slipping into difficulty. To further explain how you may trade counter trends by combining your price action trading setups with the top-down analytical strategy, permit me to provide you one more example.

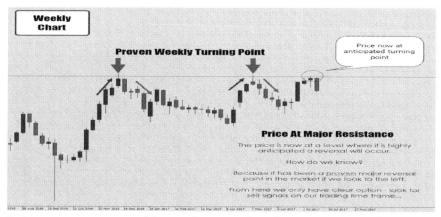

Prices are at a weekly resistance level, as seen in the chart above. Buyers were refused at this level twice, showing that the market is heated and is likely to change.

As a price action trader, you may look for a selling opportunity by going to the daily time frame. This will be a high probability setup to check whether you can identify a price action setup around the weekly resistance level on the daily time frame.

See the example below:

As you can see, the daily chart above verifies our weekly analysis; there is a solid bearish signal over the weekly barrier level. The pin bar from that level was rejected, and an inside bar phoney breakout was also manufactured.

This is a clear indicator of a trend change. Watch what transpired next:

The aforementioned example demonstrates that trading against the trend may be beneficial if it is properly mastered. As a rookie, I strongly suggest keeping with the trend and striving to practice the top-down analytical notion as much as you can. Once you have mastered trading against the trend, you may next start trading high-probability counter-trend events.

There are different strategies for planning trades and anticipating market changes, but most of these ways enhance uncertainty and reduce faith in the results.

Top-down analysis is one of the simplest tactics to comprehend if you want to trade well, and keeping the analysis uncomplicated is often the best path of action.

Open your charts and try to put everything you studied in this chapter into practice right now.

Utilize these tactics to try to determine the market trend. While it may first look a little odd, with enough screen time and knowledge, you will be able to clearly detect the market direction.

CHAPTER FOUR

TRADING STRATEGIES AND METHODS

Three essential elements of price action trading were discussed in the past chapters:

The first part focuses on market trends. You are proficient at spotting these patterns by doing research over a number of occasions. You can discern between range-limited markets and trending markets. And you are aware of how each market moves.

The second component is the level; you studied how to draw trend lines and how to show zones of support and resistance. Your capacity to better enter the market at the correct time will be strengthened by this.

The third component is the signals; you are familiar with numerous candlestick patterns and are aware of the psychology that drives their growth as well as the message they deliver. We will employ these three elements—the trend, the level, and the signal—as part of our trading approach to gain money on any financial market. I propose that you aim to deliver three key reactions when you analyze a chart:

How is the market performing?

Is the market choppy, consolidating, or trending? Whether something is trending, you can detect whether it's heading up or down. You will observe that the market is trading horizontally between two borders if it is a range market. Additionally, you close your chart and remain away if the market is sluggish.

2. What are the market's strongest levels?

You will strive to locate the most significant support and resistance levels regardless of whether the market is headed upward, downward, or in a range. The ideal levels to purchase and sell the market are at these levels.

3. What is the most trustworthy indicator to enter the market?

The finest indication to enter the market displays the best moment to carry out your acquisition.

Employing the pin bar candlestick pattern

One of the most well-known Japanese candlesticks is the pin bar, which price action traders often exploit to identify market reversal moments. You will acquire a deep understanding of the parameters necessary for high-probability setups as well as how to recognize credible pin bar signals in this portion.

A pin bar is a chart candlestick that denotes rejection and forecasts that the market will move against it. It is distinguished by its exceptionally long tail. The real body is the area between the open and close; generally, all pin bars have a modest real body and a long shadow.

While the colour of the candlestick is not extremely significant, bullish candles with a white actual body are more successful than candles with a genuine black body. A bullish pin bar is recognizable by its lower wicks, while a bearish one is defined by prolonged higher wicks. On the other side, black genuine body bearish pin bars are more crucial than white actual body ones.

See a picture of a pin bar below:

Bearish pin bars:

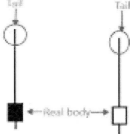

Bullish pin bars:

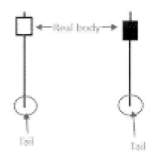

How may pin bar candlestick setups be recognized?

Great price action setups don't exist in the market, to be honest, as you will see when you occasionally uncover a high probability setup, get enthused about it, and place your trade with conviction, only to be disappointed when the signal fails for unknown reasons.

The market doesn't move according to pin bar formations; rather, the law of supply and demand regulates the market, which only happens seldom.

As an instance, if you see a quality pin bar candle at a support key level in an uptrending market, this is a significant purchase indication that you shouldn't ignore. However, if the quantity of money spent by buyers in this transaction is lower than the amount of money invested by sellers in the risk related to the same agreement, the market will not move in the way you forecast.

If the signal doesn't work, it doesn't signify that your analysis is erroneous or that pin bars don't operate; rather, it only implies that the market didn't validate your conclusion. As a result, you should accept your defeat and look for another opportunity. Why should we strive for exceptional pin bar configurations if the market doesn't appreciate them? you may be asking.

As you are aware, trading is a game of possibilities; there is no such thing as certainty. For this reason, you should assess your pin bar installations from a variety of angles. Additionally, the fact that you are hunting for high-quality setups shows that you are aiming to maximize the possibility of success, which is the ideal mentality for successful traders.

The following criteria should be examined by this price movement indication to judge whether or not a pin bar is lucrative to trade:

-The pin bar formed in greater time frames, such as the 4-hour or daily time frame, should be studied since smaller time frames quickly detect a lot of pin bar signals; these setups should be avoided because smaller time frames generate a lot of false signals. Examine the picture below:

-A pin bar that is created in line with market trends is more robust than one that is produced against it.

- If you can spot a distinct pattern, it demonstrates you are aware of the market's prevailing power.

This candlestick pattern was made practicable by the trend, which adds to its potency. Look at the graph below:

Bullish pin bars were formed in accordance with the uptrend work, as you can see in the chart above, and they should be taken into consideration.

However, it is advisable to disregard the bearish ones that were generated in opposition to the trend.

It's crucial to note that a pin bar has a certain anatomy. You can detect if a candlestick is a pin bar by calculating the distance between the real body and the tail.

Stronger pin bars have longer tails.

The psychology underpinning the design of pin bar candles

Pin bars occur when prices are rejected, but this rejection is not a foreshadowing of a reversal, as a similar price action setup may happen elsewhere on your chart.

Crucial critical levels, such as support and resistance, supply and demand zones, and moving averages, are the most significant locations to notice while trading pin bars. This candlestick chart pattern's development at these levels offers a good insight into market movement.

For instance, if the rejection comes near a support level, this is a strong indicator that the bulls are more powerful and eager to drive the market higher.

Look at the graph below:

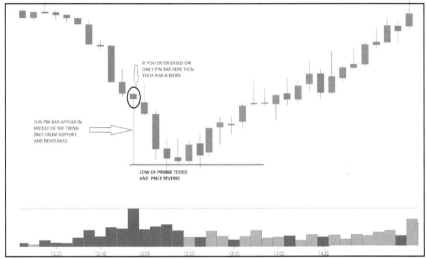

The bears are rejecting prices and preventing the bulls from breaking through this level if the development of this candlestick occurs at a resistance level. This subsequently implies that sellers are motivated to push the market down. Look at the graph below:

Understanding the psychology underpinning the emergence of this price action pattern will help you execute great trades based on high probability pin bar signals and forecast what is likely to happen in the future.

Using the trend to trade the pin bar candlestick

Pin bars that occur in moving markets present amazing trading possibilities with a high risk/reward ratio, therefore if you are a rookie trader, I strongly recommend you to continue with the trend.

You may transfer to trading range-bound markets or even counter-trends when you master trading with the end. It's simple to execute this strategy; you just start by detecting a solid uptrend or downtrend and wait for a pin bar to develop following a retreat to a support or resistance level.

See the example below:

As you can see, the price was rejected from the resistance level, demonstrating that the bears are still in command of the slide. The chart below demonstrates how this price action signal performs if it is traded with the trend.

The development of the pin bar signifies the completion of the retracement move and the initiation of the impulsive advance toward the downtrend's resistance level.

All the standards specified below are met, making this arrangement high-quality:

1. The pin bar is brilliantly developed and it follows the market's movement.

2- The rejection occurred at a vital key level, which denotes a market turning point (resistance level).

3- Trading is suggested owing to the exceptional risk-to-return ratio.

Sometimes, despite the market's movement, we are unable to draw support and resistance levels because price movements mask unchanging important levels. If this is the case, you may apply the 21-moving average, which would serve as dynamic support in an upswing and dynamic resistance in a downturn. See the image below:

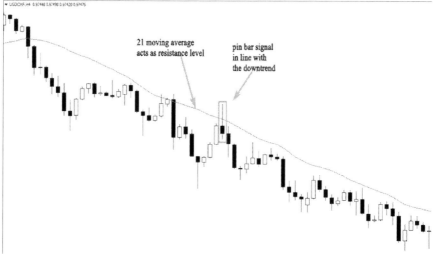

The market was sliding downward, as depicted in the image above. By applying the 21 moving averages, we may uncover dynamic resistance levels and high chance pin bar setups. View an additional graph below:

The 4-hour chart up above indicates how the 21-moving average may be able to signal up significant marketplaces for us.

The market faces purchasing pressure when prices approach close to the moving average, which pushes the price to grow.

Since the trend is bullish, the price action setup has bullish anatomy, and the rejection from the 21-moving average is a confirmation signal to buy the market, the pin bar signal is evident on the chart.

CHAPTER FIVE

TECHNIQUES FOR TRADING

When determining the level (support or resistance) and the trend (uptrend or downtrend).

Additionally, a pin bar that follows the trend may be noted at these levels. Knowing how to enter the market employing this candlestick pattern is the second step.

Depending on the candle anatomy, the market conditions, and your money management style, there are different entry choices when it comes to trading pin bars, in my experience.

1. The quick market entrance option: this approach comprises buying or selling promptly when the pin bar closes without first getting confirmation.

This strategy will help you in catching the move as it develops since, on occasion, the price increases after the pin bar shuts, and if you are not in the market, the transaction will depart without you.

See the example below:

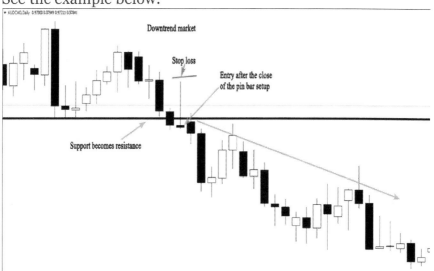

The aforementioned chart indicates how a strong entrance might help you execute your trade at the correct time without falling afoul of the market.

As you can see, we authorized this transaction as we possessed these three important components:

The market was headed south, thus we were hunting for selling possibilities.

The grade: We can detect a support level that turns to resistance in this graph.

The signal: After the retracement back to the resistance level, a clean pin bar was created. When all three of these criteria are fulfilled, you need just place your trade when the pin bar closes and your stop loss above the extended tail. In the case of a downturn, the next support level will be your profit goal. You may identify market entry with a high possibility of success by applying these three criteria.

The approach known as the cautious entry option entails entering the market when the range bar retracement has touched 50%.

This strategy will sometimes be beneficial and deliver you a risk/reward ratio that is greater than 5, but sometimes the market may move on without you. Look at the picture below:

The image above gives us an understanding of the necessity of careful entrances; as you can see, this entry style helps in decreasing risks and enhancing earnings.

The risk to reward in the aforementioned transaction is more than 5:1. To make a fair income, one deal like this each month is more than enough. View a different diagram below:

One drawback of this entry approach is that occasionally the market won't retrace to 50% of the range bar, which will leave you feeling dissatisfied because the market will continue to advance to the profit target without you. There is no erroneous or ideal entrance strategy; both perform flawlessly. However, as you accumulate experience and screen time, you will be able to pick whether to trade aggressively or conservatively.

Trading confluence pin bars

Confluence is a trading concept applied by price action traders to filter their entry locations and uncover high probability signals in the market. Confluence comes when many technical indicators deliver the same indication.

Trading with confluence is crucial regardless of your degree of competence, as it will assist you to focus on quality setups rather than quantity and drastically boost your trading results.

For instance, if we are hunting for a pin bar signal, we need to discover additional sources of confluence to corroborate our entry; we are not going to accept every pin bar that we find on our chart. Confluence denotes combination or conjunction; it is a circumstance in which two or more components merge or come together.

Factors of confluence

The trend: is one of the most significant components of confluence; experienced traders look for it first on their charts since you can't trade any setup without knowing whether it matches the market's direction or not.

In a downturn, a bearish pin bar is a more effective indicator than it is in a range-bound market. Supply and demand zones, as well as support and resistance levels, are crucial levels that are especially vital in the market since they are continually examined by all main participants.

Moving averages: I employ the 8 and 21 moving averages in my technical trading. These moving averages operate as dynamic support and resistance and are a vital component of confluence in trending markets.

Tool for measuring Fibonacci retracements: I apply the 61 percent and 50 percent Fibonacci retracements to discover the market's strongest locations.

Trend lines: Adding these lines to your charts offers you a sense of the market's direction and aids in recognizing the most significant market reversal times.

You do not need to discover all these levels while studying your chart to assess whether or not the transaction is real.

Finding merely one or two confluences that happen in conjunction with a wonderful pin bar layout is sufficient to make a profitable trade.

For example an evident pin bar indicator around support or resistance level in accordance with the direction of the market. See the image below:

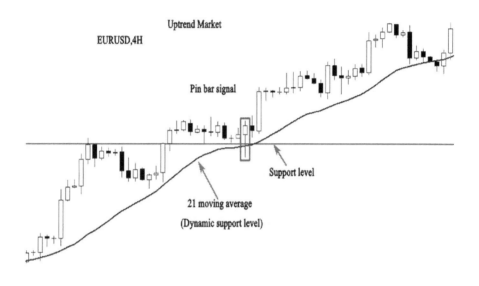

We have a high chance arrangement with four confluence components in the aforementioned case.

1. The Trend: Given that the market is trading upward, we should keep pace with it and look for a purchase chance.

2. The level: In the market, the support level is a crucially essential level.

As you can see, the price fell back to the resistance level after breaking beyond it.

3. The signal: This is the establishment of the bullish pin bar that comes after a retreat to a level of resistance that afterwards works as support.

4- Another signal: The rejection of the support level and the 21 moving average functioning as a dynamic support level are further signals. All of these components operate together to give us a solid trading indication to acquire the market.

See another example:

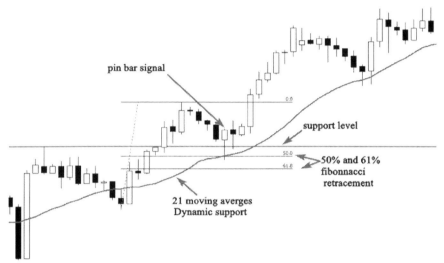

In the example below, a bullish trend and a level of resistance that afterwards became support are two of four confluent levels that together represent a large trade signal.

The 21-moving average, which functions as a dynamic support level, is the third one. and the pin bar formation, which is consistent with the bullish trend at these levels, is the last element. If you accept this trading approach, you will fundamentally transform how you see the market and begin trading like a sniper by sitting back and waiting for the finest trading possibilities to present themselves rather than pushing yourself to make trades happen.

Pin Bars Trades Examples

To help you grasp how to trade the pin bar candlestick pattern with the trend, I will supply you with a few trading instances.

and how to harness the idea of confluence to support your efforts.

See the chart below:

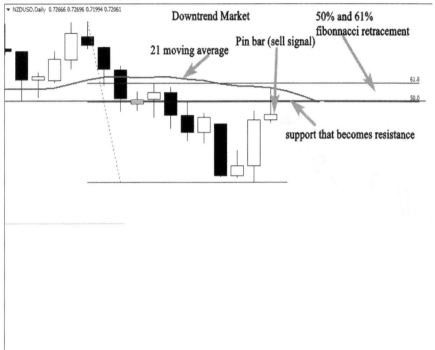

As you can see from this NZD USD daily chart, the market is sinking. This is the first piece of information we extract from the chart.

Following the price retraced back to this level after the breakout of the support level that finally turned resistance, a pin bar candlestick pattern was produced.

The development of the pin bar close to the resistance level signals the conclusion of the retracement move and the initiation of an impulsive move, which is expected to follow.

The pin bar is rejected from these levels when the 21 moving average and the Fibonacci retracement are visible on the chart, signalling that this level is extremely critical and that sellers are keen to force the market down.

We have excellent justifications in this position to sell the market, starting with the decline.

The development of the pin bar next to the resistance level, which denotes the finish of the retreat and the initiation of a new move down, is the second component.

The pin bar's rejection from the resistance level and the 21-moving average is the third factor.

The pin bar rejection from the 50% Fibonacci retracement level, one of the market's most crucial levels, is the final contributing component.

Check out the chart below to see what transpired next:

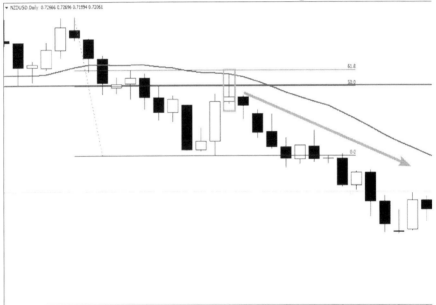

As you can see in the graph up above, our analysis was accurate and based on good evidence to enter the market.

I want you to master this strategy so that you may trade the market efficiently. View a different illustration below:

The graph above provides two key purchase possibilities.

The market was going upward, and there was a significant probability of entry when the first pin bar formed after the retreat to the support level.

The rejection from the 21-moving average and the 50 percent Fibonacci retracement serve as substantiation of our entry.

With the second pin bar, the same thing happened, allowing us to reenter the market and make further money.

Pin Bar Trading in Range-Bound Markets

When prices quit producing higher highs and lower lows and begin to trade horizontally between a set level of support and a defined level of resistance, we may say that a market is ranging.

Once I realize that the market acts differently, I must change my approaches and create a trading strategy that corresponds with the existing market circumstances.

Once I have established the range, it is quite basic to trade it by going long when prices reach the support level and going short when prices are likely to approach the resistance level. To verify a ranging market, I need to look for at least two touches of the support level and two touches of the resistance level.

An illustration of a range-bound market is shown below:

You can see that we have an opportunity to buy or sell the market as prices approach the important support or resistance level; all we have to do is search for a clear price action setup, such as a pin bar candlestick.

Look at the illustration below:

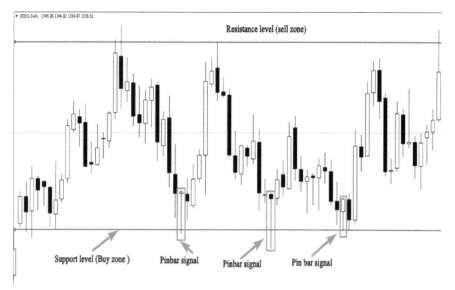

The aforementioned image presents us with three trading possibilities; allow me to explain how you may execute it profitably:

One is a pin bar that has been rejected from the support level; you may either place a buy order quickly after the pin bar closes or wait until the market approaches the centre of the pin bar range. Above the support level should be your stop loss, and towards the resistance level should be your profit target.

This trade offers an excellent risk-return ratio.

2. The second trade possibility shows itself at the support level. After the pin bar has closed, you place a buy order, and your stop loss should be below the support level. Your aim is the following resistance level.

3. The third configuration is an obvious purchase opportunity. As you can see, the market rejected the support level and created a pin bar to let us know that buyers are still there and that the market is likely to bounce back from the support level.

The simplest approach to make money trading range-bound markets is to trade from key significant support and resistance levels; never try to trade any setup if it is not firmly rejected from these zones.

The second strategy comprises either waiting for prices to retrace back to the breakout point before going long or short the market, or trading in the direction of breakouts of major crucial levels.

See the example below:

The price broke out of the support level in the previous chart and returned to the breakout point. The creation of an obvious pin bar also presents a high chance indicator to short the market.

This is how skilled traders exploit this price movement to trade range markets.

How to employ technical indicators to examine pin bar signals

I'm not encouraging you to focus on indicators to make signals as this will never work for you, but if you can combine your price action approaches with the right indicators, you will be able to filter your signals and trade the ideal settings. Using technical indications to verify your entry will raise the possibility that the transaction will be rewarding.

The Bollinger bands indicator is one of the greatest tools I employ to validate my entrance when I examine a range-bound market.

John Bollinger devised this technical trading method to evaluate market volatility.

The strategy is incredibly basic; we will combine horizontal support and resistance with the upper and lower Bollinger bands to construct a phoney breakthrough. If prices reject major support and resistance levels as well as the bands, the market is likely to rebound from these levels.

See an example below:

As the market draws close to the upper or lower bars on the above chart, prices immediately bounce. This is due to the Bollinger bands operating as dynamic support and resistance.

The rejection of a pin bar from a horizontal key level and bands is a clear indication to buy or sell the market, so if we witness this.

Trading is all about emotions, and occasionally, you may get a magnificent pin bar signal in a range-bound market, but you will find it challenging to assess whether to take a trade or ignore it. This confirmation strategy is quite basic, and it will aid you determine whether to accept a transaction or disregard it.

Setting up your Bollinger bands on your chart is all that is necessary in this case. If you observe that the signal is rejected by both the bands and the horizontal levels, don't overthink what to do next.

Simply place your order, decide on your stop loss and profit target, and then walk away and let the market take care of the rest.

See another photo below:

The daily chart up top demonstrates how this indicator may boost confident trade execution; the pin bar's erroneous violation of the resistance level was a strong hint to sell the market. The artificial breakout of the upper band also helped to legitimize the transaction.

Always employ this technical indicator in tandem with horizontal key levels and keep in mind that it should only be utilized as a confirmation tool in range-bound markets rather than to issue warnings. You will observe how this approach can enhance your trading account.

In conclusion, I strongly encourage you to put these strategies to the test before creating and funding your trading account.

CHAPTER SIX

PATTERN OF THE ENGULFING BAR CANDLESTICK

One of the most powerful and effective price action patterns is the engulfing bar pattern, which, when applied correctly as an entry signal, may drastically enhance your trading profitability.

Whether you are a newbie trader or an experienced trader hunting for a better trading approach than what you have been doing, you will discover how to apply the engulfing bar pattern effectively in this section. You have come to the proper site.

Enveloping Bar Pattern: What Is It?

This reversing candlestick pattern consists of two opposing colored bodies in which the second body engulfs or covers the first one:

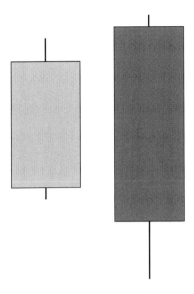

When a bullish engulfing pattern occurs near the finish of a downturn, it is a strong signal that purchase pressure has defeated selling pressure.

In other words, the buyers are now committed.

When a bullish rising comes to an end, a negative engulfing pattern occurs. This pattern is a top trend reversal indicator because it suggests that the bulls are no longer in charge of the market and that the price trend is likely to reverse.

See the illustrations below:

For this candle to be labelled a reversal pattern, according to Steve Nison, the developer of contemporary candlestick charting, it must meet three crucial criteria:

1) There is a distinct rise or decline in the market.

2 The engulfing candle consists of two candlesticks, the first of which is entirely consumed by the second.

3) The contrast between the first real body and the second actual body.

How To Trade The Price Movement Signals From Engulfing Bars?

You must respect these three important elements in order to trade this chart candlestick pattern successfully:

1. The pattern

Any chart will show you that there are instances when the market is certainly headed in one direction and other times when it is lurching sideways. The simplest way to gain money in the market is to trade the engulfing bar pattern with the trend, to be honest. To recognize whether the market is trending or not, you don't need to have a sophisticated knowledge of technical analysis.

Make it simple: If the market is displaying a pattern of higher highs and higher lows, the market is in an uptrend, and if it is establishing a series of lower highs and lower lows it is simply about a declining market.

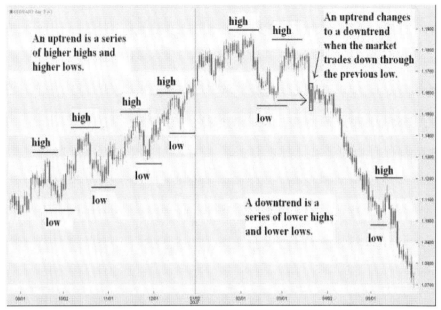

An uptrend is a series of higher highs and higher lows.

An uptrend changes to a downtrend when the market trades down through the previous low.

A downtrend is a series of lower highs and lower lows.

To judge if the market is trending or not, simply look at your chart and try to follow the rule of higher highs and higher lows and vice versa. The example above clearly demonstrates an uptrend.

Remember that the markets move in trends as you review your charts. Trading with the trend is the most crucial component of your technical analysis. There is nothing more crucial than the trend; resist attempting to prevent it or control it, since doing so will cost you dearly.

No matter how fantastic your trading approach is, you can't generate money in all market scenarios. You need to have enough patience to wait for the market to tell you which way to go.

The trend should be your closest companion, according to seasoned traders. If you want to perfect trading the engulfing bar pattern, your first rule should be to follow the market direction.

2. The level: After discovering a solid uptrend or downturn, the next stage is to establish the market's most crucial levels. I refer to the strongest opposition and support. Prices testing a support level and then stopping is an indicator that buyers are present. All market participants keep a watch on this location as it presents great purchasing possibilities. On the other hand, if prices test a resistance level and halt in an uptrend, this is a strong signal that there is market selling strength.

The following picture demonstrates how market players link with support and resistance levels:

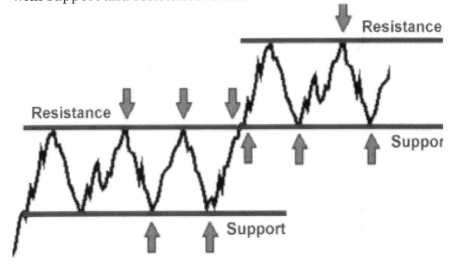

These levels may occur in a range of forms, including triangles, flags, channels, and trend lines. You'll be able to identify greater price levels in the market if you can detect them in your chart. Check out the image below to understand how to trade the engulfing bar pattern with support and resistance in a bullish or bearish trend. As prices pass through the resistance level in moving markets, that barrier may change into support.

Moving averages, Fibonacci retracement ratios, and other technical tools like supply and demand zones may also be able to lead us in the direction of the best market levels.

3. The Signal

Your ability to recognize an engulfing candlestick at a critical level in a clear uptrend or downtrend will substantially enhance the possibility of completing a good transaction. The indicator in this example is an engulfing bar pattern; you may use the same tactics while trading the inner bar candlestick pattern. Below is another illustration:

Trading the engulfing bar with moving averages

Moving average trading with the engulfing bar pattern is a very successful trading approach, but without understanding how to apply the moving average may drastically ruin your trading account.

Moving averages are used by traders in a variety of ways, including: \s-As a trend monitoring tool to determine the trend's direction, so they buy the market when prices are above the 200 simple moving average. And when the market moves below the 200 simple moving average, they sell it.

- We just investigate how prices interact with the moving averages to determine if the market is overbought or oversold. For instance, in an uptrend, if prices diverge considerably from the moving averages, this is a signal that the market is overbought.

-By applying the crossover strategy, it is possible to foresee when a trend will shift since when one moving average crosses over another, it often signifies a trend reversal. The moving averages have restrictions, just like any other trading

91

approach, which is why you need to know how to apply them effectively in the ideal market situations.

Never try to utilize this trading technical tool in range-bound or untradeable markets as it isn't suitable for all markets. Since you'll get a ton of erroneous signals, your trading account will certainly plummet. To the best of my knowledge, the easiest strategy to generate money in the market is to combine an engulfing bar pattern signal with the moving average as dynamic support and resistance in trending markets.

The strategy is quite easy; we will apply the 21 and 8-simple moving averages in the daily and 4-hour time frames, produce a clear bullish or bearish market, and then only buy when the price lowers to the moving average and an engulfing bar pattern occurs.

See the image below:

When the price retraces to the moving average, we sell. On the other hand, if the moving average is drifting downward, this signals that the market is in a negative trend.

The image below depicts how prices interact with the moving average when it operates as a dynamic resistance level and how the engulfing bar pattern signalled a high probability setup.

How to trade the engulfing bar using Fibonacci retracement

The following example depicts how the engulfing bar price movement signal fits with the 50% and 61.5% Fibonacci retracement levels. This extra signal to act on this high probability setup comes from the resistance level that transforms into support.

This kind of trading is incredibly successful, and the following example demonstrates the power of the 50% and 61.8% Fibonacci retracements:

Trading the market from the 50% and 61.8% Fibonacci levels suggests that you are trading at better price levels, which will boost the chances in your favor and help you become one of the most successful traders.

Using trendlines to trade the engulfing bar

Trend lines provide traders an understanding into the psychology of the market, notably the psychology between buyers and sellers. In addition, trend lines enable professional traders in evaluating whether the market is dismal or optimistic.

This technical trading tool may be used in a number of ways, such as to identify price and time by drawing trend lines vertically or horizontally to signify support and resistance. The application of trend lines may be done in any technique.

In trending markets, we employ fundamental trend lines to emphasize a trend by linking swing highs or swing lows in price; this strategy assists in the finding of high probability entry setups compatible with the market's overall direction. See the image below:

We constructed a trend line that functioned as resistance by connecting the extreme highs, and the formation of the engulfing bar pattern signifies a great selling opportunity.

Simply applying horizontal support and resistance levels would preclude you from completing this great trade.

It's never a bad idea to grasp how to construct trend lines because they are the simplest analytical tool you can use to investigate financial markets. It operates in all markets, including those for options, futures, commodities, and currencies.

The trend line in the previous chart acts as a level of support, and the price action signal that happened produced an outstanding buying opportunity.

How Do You Trade Sideways Markets With The Engulfing Bar?

The sideways and range markets might be among the trickiest to anticipate. The difficulty is that the markets spend more than 70% of their time in range activity, contrary to what I generally counsel traders to do.

Understanding how to approach range-bound markets is a prerequisite if you want to make a livelihood trading financial markets because if you simply focus on moving markets, you will be leaving a lot of money on the table.

What is a range-bound market?

The price begins to behave between predefined highs and lows when the market ceases creating higher highs and higher lows during an uptrend or lower highs and lower lows during a fall.

This serves as an evident indication that the market has entered a range and is no longer moving. Look at the image below:

The market is range-bound, as indicated in the example above, and is trading between horizontal support and resistance. As a result, you cannot apply the same tactics you would in a moving market to trade engulfing bar formations.

As an instance, when you are driving your car, you don't continually drive the same direction. For instance, if you are driving downtown, you strive to drive softly since you are aware that driving hastily might jeopardize your life or the lives of others.

However, since you are aware that you may drive swiftly when driving on a highway, your driving style substantially shifts. As a result, you continually seek to change your driving style to the correct circumstance.

The same is true while trading the engulfing bar pattern, as all price action approaches we previously mentioned will not be lucrative in range-bound markets, and you must apply the proper strategies that are suited for these market situations.

Before examining the greatest technique to trade trendless markets, it's crucial to recognize that not all sideways marketplaces are rewarding to trade, therefore you must be selective about trading range-bound markets to maintain your trading account. Understanding the difference between sideways and bumpy markets is crucial.

See the chart below on tough markets:

As was demonstrated above, the market trades intermittently, making it impossible for us to establish critical levels of support and resistance. Avoiding these types of markets will save you from ruining your trading account.

The first strategy will be about trading this price action pattern from critical support and resistance levels, as we see below. Trading the engulfing bar candle in a range-bound market is very basic.

The second option is to trade the breakout of the range or to wait for the retreat.

See the picture below :

Trading the false breakthrough of the important support or resistance level is the third technique.

False breakouts are one of the most successful price action tactics. They may occur in all sorts of markets, and if you know how to utilize them in combination with the engulfing bar pattern at a strong support or resistance level, you can benefit from the market by purchasing smartly at the bottoms and selling at the high.

See the image below:

Trading supply and demand zones coupled with the engulfing bar?

Zones of supply and demand are more powerful than those of support and resistance. It is the location where banks and other companies engage in the market. You will enhance your trading account if you can spot these important situations.

According to my experience, you must be able to recognize high-quality supply and demand levels on a chart in order to trade the engulfing bar pattern efficiently utilising supply and demand regions. High-quality supply and demand sectors have the following three characteristics:

1- The strength of the move: Pay specific attention to how the price exits the area; a quick evacuation of the market implies the presence of banks and other organizations.

2. Appropriate profit zone: You need to confirm that the level gives a favorable risk/reward ratio.

3. Longer time periods: The two most important supply and demand zones in the market are the daily and four-hour areas.

The chart below demonstrates a high-quality supply area. As you can see, the area moved very vigorously, which suggests that banks and other financial enterprises were there. A crucial hint that the bears are still willing to sell from the same price level was the appearance of an engulfing bar.

See another illustration of these areas:

These zones are plainly identifiable, in my perspective, because they are represented by evident motions. Significant players position their pending orders in the supply and demand sectors, and whenever the market reaches these zones, we witness a sharp movement away from these levels. This is the key to understanding supply and demand zones. Trading supply and demand zones in tandem with the engulfing bar price action indicator can enhance your likelihood of success as a trader.

Rules for Money Management in Trading

You have studied how to recognize high-probability trading setups so far, but this does not necessarily suggest that all-engulfing bar patterns are profitable to trade. Low risk/reward price action ideas must be dismissed.

There is no need to perform any extra research after the conditions for a high probability setup are established; merely ensure that your transaction has a potential of having a 2:1 risk to reward ratio. By this, I mean that the amount of money you will gain must be at least twice as great as the amount of money you would risk.

See an example below:

As you can see, the market was moving and all the parameters were completed to accept a buy order. Large demand and supply zones are the ideal price levels in sideways markets, as we have said. A strong trading opportunity arises when an engulfing bar arrives in the demand zone, but you must examine the risk/reward ratio to make sure that the transaction corresponds with your money management technique.

This technique provides a 3:1 risk to reward ratio, which enhances your chances of long-term success since if you risk $200 in this trade, you will probably gain $600. Analyzing your risk-to-reward ratio is crucially essential before making any single transaction.

Research case

Consider placing 10 transactions with a 3:1 risk/reward ratio on each one. If you succeed, you will get 600 dollars, but if the market goes against you, you will lose 200 dollars. Imagine that you only managed to win 3 transactions while losing 7 deals. Let's conduct the maths to find if you are the winner or the loser. You will lose $1400 on seven terrible transactions, but you will win 1800 on three excellent ones. As you can see, despite losing seven deals, you are still profitable. This is the financial management miracle.

The approach to entry and departure

Keep it simple, don't strive to be smarter than the other traders, and when you observe an engulfing bar pattern, you know what to look for and you are certain that the conditions are ideal to place your trade. Position an order as soon as the price action signal comes, position your stop loss below the candlestick pattern, and then only peep at the chart to identify the next level of support or resistance; this will be your profit target.

See the image below:

Don't peek back after establishing your protective stop and your aim; instead, let the market tell you whether you are right or incorrect. This will enable you to trade effectively without being swayed by your emotions.

Nobody loves to lose, particularly when it concerns money, so if the market goes against you, you will likely not feel happy. However, in the trading environment, you have to modify your mindset and realize that losing is an essential component of the game.

According to statistics, skilled traders never bet more than 2% of their equity on a single transaction. Don't take a risk of more than 1% if you are a newbie. Even if the engulfing bar pattern you see implies a high probability suggestion, don't risk more money than you can afford on a single transaction. No matter how brilliant you are, you must continuously keep probability in mind, be prepared for a streak of poor trades, and remember that if you take excessive risks with your money, you won't live long.

CHAPTER SEVEN

THE CANDLESTICK INNER BAR PATTERN

One of the strongest chart settings that expert traders search for is the inner bar candlestick pattern, yet most traders are unable to gain from it. The fundamental reasons why the majority of price action traders don't make money trading this Japanese candlestick are a lack of knowledge, ability, and lousy schooling.

An inner bar candlestick pattern is what?

Two candlesticks are used in an inside bar; the mother candle, which is the biggest of the two and is placed outside the mother bar, is the larger of the two.

Inside bar at the bottom

mother candle

inside candle

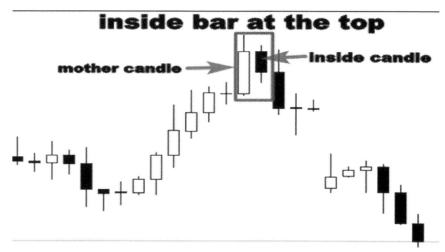

As illustrated in the following photo, which has inner bars at both the top and bottom, the second little bar is entirely engulfed by the first, which is the opposite of the engulfing bar pattern.

Since it implies that the market trend is likely to shift, the inner bar is seen as a reversal pattern, especially when it is positioned around peaks or bottoms. In markets that are moving fast, it is often seen as a continuing indicator.

Thomas Bulkowski, a seasoned trader and investor with over thirty years of market expertise, contends that: A, a bearish inside bar pattern in a bull market may, on occasion, forecast a bearish reversal in around 65% of circumstances. Additionally, around 52% of the time during a bull market, gives a good continuing signal.

Additionally, he argues that a bullish abandoned newborn is identified as a bullish reversal pattern 70% of the time in bull markets and 55% of the time in negative markets.

The Psychology Behind The Creation Of Patterns

In a bullish trend, the inner bar formation denotes a moment of consolidation; in this example, a moderate black candle on the second day after a significant increase implies that bulls are not buying any more.

Additionally, a moderate white candle following a significant decline in price during a negative trend shows that sellers are no longer in charge of the market.

Understanding the psychology driving this pattern might make it easier for you to detect crucial market turning moments and the ideal timing to enter and quit the market.

How Do You Trade Candlestick Patterns With Inner Bars?

In trending markets, the inner bar may be traded successfully, especially if the market is moving fast and the creation of this price pattern allows you a good opportunity to participate in the major advance.

This strategy needs just that you recognize a significant trend and wait for the appearance of an inner bar pattern that corresponds to the market's direction. You may enter the market at the best time and make huge gains since the formation of this pattern signals that the market will halt before making its next move.

See the picture below to learn more:

As can be seen above, the market is declining, and the inner bar pattern creation provided us three choices to follow the trend.

If you develop adapted to our method of trading, you will just seek to sell opportunities. By doing this, you are not competing with big corporations or central banks; rather, you are merely trading in the direction that the market favours.

Following the pattern's breakout, as indicated in the chart above, you may place a sell order. Your stop loss order should be positioned above the mother candle. You aim to earn the following amount of money.

See another example below:

Since you are not going to take all of these signs into account, we can see from the prior chart how efficiently this price action setting operates as a continuation pattern.

You must seek for big patterns that form in critical regions of the market, such as pivot points, moving averages, Fibonacci retracement levels, and support and resistance levels. Don't worry, we'll learn about the important trading instruments we'll need to employ in combination with inside bar setups to make the greatest trading selections.

How should I trade the inner bar breakout with resistance and support?

If you don't focus on the most critical components of technical analysis, such as support and resistance levels, it may become exceedingly complex.

Let me give you an example of how these parts indicate the psychological level at which the game is played between buyers and sellers:

If selling dominates purchasing, the price will fall below the support level. Some consumers could be scared of losing money after realizing the support level has been violated. They will consequently go out and sell the market once again to make up for their loss.

When you analyze your chart as a trader, you will observe that the support level has broken and the bears are in possession of the market. If you have a strong grasp of support and resistance levels, this is a fantastic selling opportunity, right? The difficulty is, when is the optimal timing to enter the market?

One of the most reliable price movement indicators, the inner bar pattern will advise you when it's time to enter the market and make a profit. Once you understand how to employ it in connection to these levels, you will be able to properly realize what the market is attempting to tell you and make sensible trading choices.

See the chart below:

The graphic below demonstrates how sellers broke through the support level; the formation of the inner bar pattern after this level was broken implies caution in the market.

Since it is now unsure if the support level has been broken, selling in the market quickly after its breakout would indicate an aggressive entrance, which is tricky and risky given that the breakout has not yet been validated.

But if you are skilled with trading within bars and are aware of the psychology that drives their development, you will be aware that the most secure entry should be after the pattern has broken out.

The breaking out of this candlestick pattern offers a convincing signal that the market is no longer in an uncertain position and that sellers are firmly in command. See another example

The aforementioned graph demonstrates how market participants interact with different levels and how the resistance level operates as a barrier.

The market has struggled to go over; this horizontal level inhibits customers from climbing up any farther. However, purchasers broke past the barrier level on the third attempt.

What's noteworthy is what transpired after the breakthrough; if you take another look at the chart, you'll discover that an apparent inner bar pattern has evolved there. Remember that an inner bar formation signifies uncertainty and hesitation, so the emergence of this price action pattern shows that the breakout is not yet established.

Therefore, you must exercise prudence and comprehend the risk of a false breakout occurrence.

Your full grasp of how this pattern functions will set you apart from other traders. For example, if you look at the chart above, you'll note that the ideal timing to place a buy order is after the breakout of the inner bar pattern, not after the breakout of the horizontal level.

How to trade inner bar price action setups: Some Tips

1 - Trade the greater time periods

I have nothing against trading on shorter time frames; for example, you could trade this setup on a 5 minute chart while applying other technical indicators to filter your signals and pick the high probability settings.

But in order to trade this signal, you must be an experienced trader; if you are a novice, we urge you to stick to trading in time frames other than the daily and the four-hour time frame. Trading this setup on a shorter time frame may boost your potential to accept low probability price action signals and overtrade the market. And adopting this strategy is the quickest way to lose all of your trading money. Simply focused on longer time horizons can assist you to set and forget your transaction rather than having the market impact your emotions.

2- Trade the primary trend.

If the market is in a strong bullish or bearish trend, you should start trading inside bars in that direction. If you are a rookie, never try to trade the market against the trend. You may go on to trade range-bound markets and counter-trends if you feel comfortable trading this pattern paired with the trend.

3- Only trade from significant levels

Keep in mind that not all inside bars are favorable; rather, there are select instances when this pattern flourishes. As a result, take caution to place your signal at a vital period in the market.

4- Locate various confluence-related factors.

Confluence-based trading requires incorporating various signals to arrive at the optimum trade conclusion. You must hunt for a period in the market when two or more levels are converging and wait for a clear signal to materialize in order to trade employing this strategy. You will experience more confidence in your trading strategy and be able to prevent over-trading thanks to this trading method.

How do you trade the inner bar candlestick pattern's false breakout?

Have you ever confidently placed an order anticipating a market surge, only to have the price hit your stop loss before it started to move in the direction you anticipated? Although that happened to me and I was very disappointed, this happens routinely on the market.

Banks and other financial organizations may easily steal money from us because they are aware of how we trade the market, how we think, and where we position our stop losses and profit goals. The stop loss hunting method is one of the most frequent strategies adopted by major players to extract money from inexperienced traders.

This approach entails pushing prices to a specific level where there are significant stop loss orders with the purpose of producing liquidity because the market wouldn't move without it. The market reacts aggressively in the projected direction when stop losses are realized.

One of the most remarkable candlestick patterns that demonstrates how powerful financial institutions affect the market is the inner bar false breakout pattern. Recurring patterns in the market are produced by the interaction between experienced traders and beginners.

Understanding this recurring setup and being able to identify it on your charts will help you exploit it more effectively to earn money rather than falling prey to market makers' and banks' manipulations.

This price action signal is formed when the price leaves the inner bar pattern and promptly turns around to close within the mother bar's range.

See the image below:

Bearish inside bar false breakout

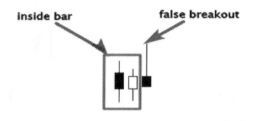

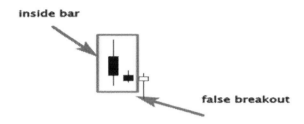

There are two variants of this price action pattern, as you can see:

While it happens close to a strong support or resistance level, a bullish inside bar fake breakout is considered as a bullish reversal signal and originates while the market is falling.

In a positive trend, a bearish inner bar false breakout develops, and when it is noticed close to a significant level in the market, it is considered as a bearish reversal pattern.

If traded with the trend, this setup may be regarded as a continuation pattern.

Examples of Inside Bars Fake Breakouts in Trading

According to my personal experience, the following levels are the most crucial ones for traders to keep a watch on while trading this signal:

-Levels of support and resistance, as well as zones of supply and demand

-The 50 percent and 61 percent retracement levels of the Fibonacci sequence.

-21 trend lines and moving averages in trending markets

-Horizontal levels in markets with range constraints

Here is an instance of trading inside bars during a phoney breakthrough in a market that is moving:

The market was heading downward, as you can see in the chart above, which implies that sellers are in command of the market. As a result, if you elected to sell the market at the resistance level, all possibilities would be in your favor.

The problem is when to enter the market, though. Where should I place my stop loss?

The market will accept your stop loss and move in the appropriate direction if you aggressively enter the market before the mother candle breaks out and put your stop loss above it.

See the image below:

If your stop loss was around the resistance level, you would also be out, and if you don't understand why, it's simply because you were a victim of the massive players chasing stops method, as described earlier, which leads the market to crash.

Knowing how to trade the inside bar fake breakout will assist you to detect market manipulation when it occurs and to profit from it rather than being caught up in the market's traps. See the picture below:

The inner bar false breakout gave us an excellent selling opportunity, as was previously indicated. There should be no reason not to take the job if you can recognize this setup and comprehend the psychology involved.

Trading exploiting Fibonacci retracements to minimize bar false breakouts

I'm not sure if you are conscious of this technical trading methodology, but I'll try to explain how to employ it in conjunction with the inside bar fake breakout in a simple and rewarding way.

What you must recognize is that the market makes impulsive swings and pullbacks during an upswing or a fall. The Fibonacci retracement aids us in discovering the market's most crucial downturn levels. The 50 percent and 61 percent Fibonacci retracement levels are the finest ones to utilise, and in my experience, these are the levels that seasoned traders pay the most attention to on their charts.

Our technique is straightforward: if the market rises strongly, we pick the technical tool on our chart and seek for retracements. If the retreat approaches levels of 50% or 61%, all we need is a price action indication to verify our admission. See the picture below:

If you study the chart above without applying this technical trading tool, you wouldn't know why the market plummeted after the retreat. By putting it into your strategy, you will be able to recognize likely trading set-ups in the market.

As seen in earlier chapters, the pin bar, inner bar, and engulfing bar setups may all be traded with the Fibonacci tool. The trade indicated above is incredibly advantageous because of the vast number of confluent factors that push us to set a sell order.

The inner bar false breakout is the third reason. The first factor is the trend, which is certainly down. The second reason is the significant Fibonacci ratios, which suggest a resistance level. To create a decent trading option, you must hunt for several triggers that support your investigation. By doing this, you will enhance your chances of success.

Consider the following hypothetical transaction:

As you can see, the price increased dramatically before drawing back to reach our key ratios and then soaring again. This area's construction of the inner bar fake breakthrough implies that the retreat is completed and another major advance is going to happen.

Knowing how to exploit the market structure to your advantage is crucial. If the market is trending, you may trade the inside bar fake breakout as we previously mentioned.

On the flip hand, you must change your plan if the market is changing. See the image below:

If you enter the market as soon as it breaks out from the inner bar and the resistance level in the preceding chart, you will be locked in a phoney breakout. This is because the market is trading between horizontal support and resistance levels.

Amateurs wanted to foresee the early breakout of the inner bar and the horizontal level in order to identify the top, but the market misled them and set up a bull trap, which resulted in the false breakout. If you find this pattern on your chart and recognize that buyers were tricked by sellers, don't hesitate to join this trade since it has a superb risk/reward ratio and is extremely profitable.

After the break bar has closed, you place a sell order, setting your stop loss above it, with the next support level as your profit target.

Keep in mind that a fake breakthrough doesn't occur every time, and that not all false breakouts are lucrative trading. This approach is not difficult, but it demands time and energy to construct.

The benefits of trading the inner bar candlestick pattern's false breakout include:

If you can uncover this trend, you'll be able to avoid stuck traders and enter the market when beginners are forced to depart with a loss.

The risk-reward of this signal has tremendous potential, as the market moves strongly when large players surprise newbies and seize their money. If you can precisely judge what transpired, you will enter at the appropriate time and make enormous profits, but this strategy is not the holy grail, and you must be ready to accept some failed trades.

Consider placing a bet of, say, 50 points to earn 400 points. By applying this price action strategy, you may study how banks and other financial organizations trade the market and anticipate correct market turning periods in advance.

Examples of Trades

To help you in understanding how to trade the market employing all the methods covered in the prior chapters, I'll offer you a number of trading examples in this section. See the first example below:

The market is decreasing, as illustrated in the figure above. As a price action trader, I will therefore try to follow this trend and hunt for important signals at the most strong critical levels.

A pin bar that was rejected from a support level that eventually turned resistance is the first signal we observed.

The rejection of the pin from the 50% Fibonacci retracement is the second point in favor of our option to sell the market.

The rejection of the pin bar from the 21 moving average, which was operating as a dynamic resistance level, is the third factor that compels us to act on this signal.

The second indication was an engulfing bar candlestick pattern, which was formed at a resistance level in line with the market trend, as you can see in the chart.

Using our price action indicators, you may trade trending markets in the fashion described above. Finding the trend and the critical levels is uncomplicated; they may be support or resistance levels, moving averages of 21 and 50 and 61 percent, or Fibonacci retracements.

Then, depending on the market's trend, wait for one of the following to form at these levels: a pin bar, an engulfing bar, an inside bar, or an inside bar false breakout. It's not challenging.

See another example below:

The market is moving horizontally between the support and resistance levels, as seen in the chart above. Since this market differentiates fundamentally from trending markets, it necessitates a separate trading method. In range markets, we trade from the boundaries, that is, from levels of support and resistance. Never try to trade inside the range.

Two significant signs developed in the chart above: the first was a pin bar that was forcefully rejected from the resistance level, and the second was an inner bar that was generated close to the support level.

See another graphic below:

There are three main pin bar signals, as indicated in the chart above. Sellers impede buyers and produce a pin bar when the market hits the 21 moving average, which functions as a resistance level and allows us a solid entry position.

Financial Management Strategies

Now that you have the strategies, you are able to assess the market, select when to purchase, sell, and leave as well as when to keep away from it.

You need to know this as a merchant, but you still don't have the castle's key. the strategy for managing money. The most critical problem that traders avoid addressing is money management. This is what differentiates winners from losers in trading.

Trading without a money management plan is basically a waste of time and resources. Because nothing will work for you, even if you have the world's most brilliant trading system. The mass of traders focus on how to enter the market and spend months or even years hunting for the correct strategy. I want you to think differently from them if you want to become a successful trader.

Position Sizing in Financial Management

Position size, or the number of lots you are risking with each transaction, is one of the most crucial components of money management.

Small lots are currently the usual position size given by all forex brokers. A micro lot may be obtained for as cheap as $1. Some forex brokers provide 10 cents for a tiny lot, which presents a possibility for traders without larger accounts; they may start with 250 dollars and nonetheless have an opportunity to develop it.

Position size should be indicated in units of dollars rather than pips. Assume you swapped 3 small lots of CAD/USA, which suggests you got or sold our dollars for 30.000. You stand to gain money equal to $3 for each pip if the market moves in your favor. You would have won $60 if you made 20 pip.

Let's split it down: 1 normal lot is similar to around $10 for each pip. Additionally, 1 micro lot is comparable to 10 cents, and 1 mini lot is worth nearly $1 for each pip. If you open a tiny trading account, you should examine the dollars at risk rather than the pip movements. Assume you set a stop loss of 50 pip and a profit aim of 100 pip. Accordingly, if the market reaches your stop loss, you will lose 50 pips, or $50, and if it fulfils your profit target, you will earn $100.

Whether you have a normal or micro account, as well as how many lots you are trading, determine the size of your position. You need to know this information as it will assist you determine how much money you are willing to risk on each trade.

The Risk-To-Reward Ratio

The guideline of the risk-to-reward ratio will determine if you succeed over the long run. Before beginning any transaction, you must calculate the amount of money you will gain if the market moves in your favor and the amount of money you will lose if it does not. Avoid entering into a contract when the reward is less than the amount at risk.

Risk to reward is 1:2, so if you were to risk $100, for instance, you would want to gain at least $200. Consider placing 10 transactions at a risk-to-profit ratio of 1:2. You run a $100 per transaction risk. You made 5 trade wins and 5 trade losses. Therefore, you will lose $500. However, you will make $1000. the advantage is $500 as a result.

You shouldn't assume that you need to win every transaction to become a successful trader since this is the power of the risk-to-reward ratio. You will always be lucrative if you exploit the risk-to-reward ratio to your advantage.

How Crucial A Stop Loss Is

Stops are a feature of all excellent approaches. When prices move in the opposite direction to a set price, a protected stop loss is an order to close out a long or short position. The stop loss must be utilized in some form since it protects against a typically severe loss.

You may establish an initial stop loss with your order on the trading platform, and the trade will be swiftly cancelled when the stop loss is obtained. Stops are a feature of all excellent approaches. When prices move in the opposite direction to a set price, a protected stop loss is an order to close out a long or short position.

The stop loss must be utilized in some form since it protects against a typically severe loss. You may establish an initial stop loss with your order on the trading platform, and the trade will be swiftly cancelled when the stop loss is obtained.

Never consider applying mental stops since you have no influence over the market and no methods of anticipating what the market will do. Consider your anticipated profits and losses before getting into a trade. Order a stop loss and place it. and your financial objective. And put your career aside.

Never Take A Risk With Money You Can't Afford To Lose.

Many traders contacted me with queries on how much capital they need to start trading. You must handle trading like a business first. In this industry, you may win money or you can lose everything.

The amount of money you need to begin trading depends on how much you can afford to lose. Never take out a loan or put a lot of money at risk that you can't afford to lose. Because trading is completely dependent on emotions, if you trade out of fear of losing your trading account, you won't succeed as a trader. primarily because your selections when trading will be affected by your emotions.

You won't be able to stick to your trading approach, and you'll undoubtedly lose money. Start simply, make an effort to get as much experience as you can, and gradually build your trading account. Successful traders generate their success in this manner.

CONCLUSION

Congratulations! If you have made it this far, it proves that you have the dedication necessary to flourish in this field. You may employ the price action strategies I've taught you to generate money trading financial markets for the rest of your life.

Your effectiveness as a trader is irrelevant to your degree of education; you may be a physician, an attorney, or a medical researcher. You risk blowing out your whole trading account if you don't abide by the recommendations.

Trading involves dedication and hard practice, just like developing a new ability. As an illustration, let me explain that it takes at least three years to earn a degree from a university. If you are sufficiently serious and dedicated, you may get your degree by waking up early every morning, studying hard, and keeping up with your studies.

The same is true for trading; if you are disciplined enough and devote the time and effort needed to learn, you will obtain the talents necessary to support your family and yourself for the rest of your life and attain financial independence. So, you won't ever contemplate obtaining a day job.

Some traders require more than 10 years to construct a strong strategy and become wealthy, while others need 20 years to make no improvement.

Fortunately, with you, this won't be the case. Since you have the map and the strategy, you won't spend time experimenting with fresh indications and techniques for years.

You already have everything you need; all you need is time to master these tactics. Give yourself some breathing room and invest as much time as you can in your education since this is the only way to excel in this field.

You will construct these trading methods over time as you realize what works and what doesn't for you. Don't think in terms of creating money as fast as possible; instead, focus on being an expert in what you do, and money will follow you wherever you go. Keep practicing and learning from your blunders.

Best of luck.

Made in the USA
Las Vegas, NV
06 November 2024

11219775R00074